# Scandi Christmas

## WELCOME

There's no time quite like Christmas time to embrace *hygge* in your home! In this brand new title, we'll share some of our favourite Scandinavian-inspired homes at Christmas, and reveal how these homeowners embrace the Nordic way of life over the festive period. We've also shared dozens of Scandi-themed crafts to make your house a rustic retreat, including unique advent calendars and chic homemade cards, as well as delicious dishes to share with friends and family. We'll also explore how to channel the Scandi mindset over the season, from how to reduce stress and budget for the festivities, to escaping all hectic duties and planning a Scandinavian trip to winter wonderland!

The content in this book is aimed at providing inspiration for furniture, decorating, and storage solutions that can work in your home. Specific products are referenced within the book as a guide only – while the trends, prices and availability of products was correct at the time of original publication, please be aware this information is subject to change.

FROM THE MAKERS OF
Ideal Home

# Contents

| | | | |
|---|---|---|---|
| 6 | **HOW TO STYLE CHRISTMAS THE SCANDI WAY** From nature-led décor to timeless traditions, bring a little Scandinavian magic into your home | 38 | **IT'S TIME TO EMBRACE THE COLD** Forget doom and gloom – we reveal the latest wellbeing trend for making the most of winter |
| 12 | **SEASONAL SCANDI** Bring the outdoors in with this pared-back style that promotes seasonal wellness through mood-boosting greenery | 40 | **FESTIVE FLAIR** Christmas is a modern affair in Katie's family home, with the decorations chiming with the Scandi-influenced décor |
| 16 | **WINTER WONDERLAND** Take your Scandi festivities up a notch with a unique Christmas trip to the Nordics | 46 | **CARD TRICKS** Want to make Christmas that little bit extra-special? Look no further than our simple ideas for one-of-a-kind cards |
| 22 | **GOOD TIDINGS** Serendipity played a part in Alex and Chelsea being able to build this gorgeous home from scratch | 52 | **SCANDI-LUXE COOL YULE** Embrace a chic twist on classic Scandi seasonal style |
| 32 | **ALTERNATIVE ADVENT** Create an extra-special lead up to the festivities by making your own unique hand-crafted Advent calendar and let the countdown to Christmas begin! | 58 | **"I LOVE RUSTIC SCANDI STLYE"** The neutral monochromes of Tracy's home are sprinkled with textural seasonal details for a luxe festive look |
| | | 68 | **SCANDI INSPIRED DISHES** Whether it's a simple snack or luxurious cake, try these delightful dishes to make your Christmas truly Scandinavian |

# Contents

74 **CHRISTMAS WREATH** Welcome guests with a fresh flower and pine cone arrangement hung on your door

76 **HOW TO REDUCE SEASONAL STRESS** We speak to the experts for their tips on keeping things simple for a happier festive time this year

79 **BUDGETING FOR THE FESTIVE SEASON** Kalpana Fitzpatrick shares her financial wisdom on getting a grip on your festive budget and reining in your debt hangover

80 **LINE OF BEAUTY** Interior designer Justin transformed a characterless 1930s house, creating a more spacious, welcoming home

90 **CHRISTMAS GATHERING** Collect pine fronds, branches and berries for a rustic Scandi-style Christmas in seasonal shades of red, white and green

96 **HANDCRAFTED CHRISTMAS** Get creative over the holidays with easy-to-make ideas for lights, decorations and festive trimmings

102 **WHITE CHRISTMAS** Emma and Ant's elegant and timeless home may be all serene shades of cream and white, but it doesn't mean it's not made for festive family fun

112 **THE PERSONAL TOUCH** Get crafty with edible decorations this Christmas – perfect for decorating the house or gifting to friends and family

116 **IT'S A WRAP** Be inspired and get creative with our six stylish 'no-waste' wrapping ideas – from brown paper packages to gifts tied in fabric off-cuts, the results are beautiful and sustainable

122 **THE A-Z OF SCANDI BRANDS** From iconic chairs to sleek storage and elegant kitchenware, these brands champion Scandinavian design

# HOW TO STYLE Christmas the Scandi way

From nature-led décor to timeless traditions, here's how to bring a little Scandinavian magic into your home this Christmas

When it comes to creating a cosy home that really sings Christmas, few design aesthetics capture the mood quite like Scandi interior style. Rooted in simplicity, comfort and a love of natural materials, the Scandinavian approach lends itself perfectly to the festive season. In contrast to some cultures that go big on glitz and sparkle, this ethos is about a more understated kind of magic – one that feels calm, inviting and deeply homely.

At the heart of Scandi design is the concept of *hygge* – the Danish idea of warmth and contentment – and Christmas offers the perfect excuse to embrace it. Think pared-back palettes of soft whites and greys, layered with natural textures like wood, wool and linen. Add in the glow of candles, twinkling fairy lights and lashings of greenery, and the result is an interior that feels effortlessly festive, without ever tipping into excess.

'Christmas in Scandinavia is about embracing slow living and the warmth of *hygge*,' says Kristina Kirkegaard, Head of Design at Sostrene Grene. 'It's a slow-paced, mindful way of celebrating, which values togetherness and simplicity. There's something uniquely comforting about Scandinavian interiors at Christmas. Thoughtful details, whether handmade decorations, candlelight, or a cosy corner to unwind, bring moments of peace and beauty into the home, making Scandi style feel timeless.'

> **'Decorations are SIMPLE, TACTILE and often HANDMADE'**

This style is also wonderfully practical for busy homes. Stripped-back décor means you can focus on cosy corners, rustic tables dressed with simple evergreens, and decorations that feel handmade and heartfelt.

'With its homespun touches and history-rich traditions, Scandinavian style exudes warmth and cosiness,' adds designer Reena Simon, author of *Scandi Rustic* and founder of @hygge_for_home. 'By borrowing and leaning into these traditions, we can bring more meaning and magic into our own festive season, making Christmas not just about one day, but about a whole month of moments to cherish.'

Here's how to channel Scandi style and festive traditions to create your own winter wonderland this Christmas.

## Keep it calm

If you're keen to create a Scandi-inspired Christmas space, leave any gaudy glitters, vivid colours and sparkling tinsels safely stashed in the loft. Instead, think crisp whites, soft greys and warm neutrals, layered with plenty of greenery and subtle accents of muted red, brass or even soft blush. Decorations are simple, tactile and often handmade: delicate paper stars, origami-style baubles, ceramic houses and carved wooden figures that nod to folklore. Garlands of eucalyptus or fir bring freshness, while woven hearts, clay tags and fabric stockings in natural linen or wool add texture and charm.

'Scandi festive decor feels integrated into your interior, rather than added on,' explains Reena

Søstrene Grene's 2025 Christmas collection embraces the beauty of nature to make your home feel like a winter wonderland

Get the family involved in decorating your tree with simple, timeless bows and baubles from Søstrene Grene

Simon. 'While in Britain we often decorate as a "big reveal", Scandinavians weave festive touches into the everyday, enhancing what's already there in quiet, beautiful ways. Instead of filling a home with glitter and novelty, the focus tends to be on celebrating nature and tradition. Fresh spruce branches are placed in vases, while straw ornaments and paper stars hang in windows. The dining table itself becomes central, layered with natural linens, ceramics and an abundance of candlelight, designed for lingering meals and conversation.' For more Scandi-inspired design inspiration, check out Reena's online course with Create Academy (createacademy.com).

## 'Be inspired by nature

At the heart of Scandi style is a deep connection with nature, and this link feels especially powerful at Christmas. In the Nordics, the long, dark winters mean interiors are designed to be bright, nurturing and in harmony with the great outdoors.

During the festive season, this ethos comes alive with natural touches that bring freshness and calm into the home. Lush fir branches, sprigs of eucalyptus and pine cones are gathered to decorate tables, mantels and doorways, while simple wreaths, wooden ornaments and paper garlands echo organic shapes. The result is a festive look that feels totally in tune with the season.

'Scandinavian festive décor is often nature led,' explains Reena. 'To create your own winter wonderland, think foraged branches, scattered pine cones, greenery styled simply in vases and white hyacinth blooms on the table.'

So, let the great outdoors be your inspiration. Embrace the winter chill and gather armfuls of foliage, from white-berried mistletoe to soft pussy willow and glossy holly leaves. Arrange it in vases, on mantelpieces and shelves, or weave it through circular wreaths. Ivy, firs and evergreens also look beautiful entwined around your bannisters, while pine cones look pretty scattered in stoneware bowls.

When it comes to your dining table, consider adding subtle sprinkles of trailing ivy, dried fruit or even walnuts along your runner. To keep the look elegant and understated, aim for crackers, napkins and tablecloths in neutral hues, then add simple pillar candles in creamy tones.

Natural scents are also a powerful way to bring the outside in, and amplify the festive feel. Add sprigs of aromatic eucalyptus to a vase or to your tablescape. Potted white hyacinths or narcissi also add texture and an incredible scent. Pot them in a woven basket or terracotta container, and top the soil with a carpet of moss. 'When choosing your Christmas tree, opt for a fragrant variety like the Norway Spruce and the smell will be akin to a Scandinavian forest,' adds Reena.

## How to style Christmas the Scandi way

## Creating a COSY, UPLIFTING atmosphere indoors is ESSENTIAL

Festive room sprays, candles and diffusers are all great ways to evoke a sense of the natural world inside. Spritz fragrances and light candles in crisp pine, spruce, eucalyptus or soft woody cedar, and layer with warming notes of clove, cinnamon or cardamom for subtle Christmas cosiness.

### 'Layer your light

It's no accident that lighting is one of the most important elements of Scandinavian design – and at Christmas, it comes into its own. In the depths of winter, much of Scandinavia sees only a couple of hours of daylight, so creating a cosy, uplifting atmosphere indoors is essential. Harsh overheads and stark spotlights are firmly avoided; instead, Scandi interiors are known for their gentle schemes that layer light using a combination of standard lamps, table lamps, ceiling pendants and task lights. Colour temperature matters too – cool, clinical light is out, and a soft golden glow is in.

At Christmas, this translates into interiors that feel cocooning and atmospheric. Paper star lanterns glowing in windows are a Scandi staple, casting a soft radiance that also looks beautiful from outside. Clusters of tealights or candles in simple holders instantly create intimacy on tables and mantels, while hurricane lamps or lanterns placed by the front door create a home that glows with comfort and cheer, even in the darkest months of the year.

When it comes to lighting your Christmas tree itself, Reena advises against adding too much twinkle. 'The "less is more" ethos is favoured in Scandinavia,' she explains. 'So much so, that Christmas trees can be decorated with or without lights. If you're using them, stick to a light touch and opt for warm white tones for the ultimate *hyggelig* feeling.'

### 'Think organic

Scandi design champions the use of natural materials, and these really come to the fore during the festive season. From tactile woollen throws and soft sheepskins to illuminated paper stars and felted decorations, organic fabrics help to foster homely Christmas vibes. Increase that serene sense of warmth by draping chunky knitted blankets across benches and sofas, and hanging up simple hessian stockings beside the fireplace.

When it comes to your Christmas tree, avoid weighing down branches with attention grabbing or gaudy baubles. Instead, aim for simple ornaments in natural materials. If your decorations need a refresh, seek out pieces that feel natural and timeless. Ornaments made from wood, paper, felt, glass or even ceramic add texture, without overpowering the tree itself. Avoid anything overly glittery or fussy; instead, choose designs with clean lines and organic shapes that echo nature, such as stars or snowflakes. The beauty of this style is its longevity – classic pieces you'll bring out year after year.

'Every year, the Danish brand Georg Jensen launches silver or gold-plated ornaments,' adds Reena Simon. 'This might sound lavish, but style comes first and the designs are always simple and traditional, making use of shapes like hearts, trees and stars. The metal finish offers a soft, warm glow, which stands out against the tree's greenery.'

When it comes to designing your tree, Reena recommends tackling it from the bottom up. 'The Christmas tree is at the heart of the Scandi festive season,' she says. 'Start by thinking about the stand – you'll find lovely understated star-shaped bases from Danish brands such as Skagerak.

'For decorations, take inspiration from nature. A Scandinavian Christmas is steeped in history that encompasses many traditions, so avoid anything too "on trend". In Scandinavia, the wintry landscapes set the tone and draw to create a contemporary calming, earthy colour palette. Use soft neutral shades from whites, greys, greens and a splash of gold to bring your Christmas tree to life.' Of course, a pop of Nordic red and white also doesn't go amiss.

### 'Take time to craft

Scandinavians prize togetherness, and Christmas is a great opportunity to slow down and get crafty, or be creative in the kitchen. 'Christmas is truly the season of *hygge* and, for Scandinavians, the festive season is less about big events and more about the everyday moments that bring people together,' says Sostrene Grene's Kristina Kirkegaard. 'This could be lighting a candle each day to count down the days until Christmas,

# How to style Christmas the Scandi way

delighting the little ones with small surprises to make the wait for Christmas feel a little sweeter and shorter, crafting decorations with loved ones, or simply taking time to enjoy a quiet moment with a cup of *glogg* (spiced mulled wine) or tea.'

Slow, mindful activities like baking and crafting add soul to the festive season, as well as focusing the mind on quality time with family and friends. Reena Simon adds, 'The Scandinavian festive season is less about doing more, and more about savouring the moment. This slow-living approach might look like baking *lussekatter* (sweet buns flavoured with golden saffron and raisins) together, or taking a snowy walk before returning to a candlelit home.

'Interiors are arranged to support this slower pace of life, with seating pulled close to the fire, blankets draped for comfort, and lamps softening every corner. *Hygge* turns the home into a calm and tactile sanctuary and ensures that even in the darkest month of the year, there's light, warmth, and joy in abundance. By stripping away the excess, you create space for rituals that matter, whether that's gathering with family, sharing food or just enjoying the simplicity and steadier pace of December days.'

If you're keen to get crafty, tree decorations are the perfect way to get everyone on board. 'When it comes to decorating your tree, do get the family involved,' urges Reena. 'So many decorations can be handmade from paper, branches, straws and other natural materials. If you need inspiration or "how to" videos, YouTube is a great place to start.'

Danish paper cones, or "*kræmmerhuset*", are a simple project suitable for most ages. They're also loved by children, because they get filled with treats! Simply roll a piece of sturdy paper or card into a cone shape, then glue handles on the inside and hang from your Christmas tree. 'Use linen cloth, wire or ribbon for the handles,' suggests Reena. 'Then fill them with homemade baked biscuits or treats. It's about creating something personal and unique.'

## 'Revel in rituals

Of course, annual traditions are a great way to enhance this spirit of togetherness, and will usher in some serious festive feels. 'Scandinavians create a warm and welcoming atmosphere by celebrating simple, meaningful traditions, such as lighting the candle and counting the days until Christmas, decorating the Christmas tree with family, or welcoming the little, invisible elf into the home during the festive season – a fun tradition for both children and adults,' says Kristina Kirkegaard. 'These traditions invite a shared way of celebrating, which centres on togetherness and comfort.'

For Reena, the festive buildup begins with Advent. 'My personal favourites are Advent rituals,' she says. 'I enjoy lighting a candle each Sunday, or making handmade calendars filled with small, thoughtful surprises. It's about togetherness over excess, and embracing the idea that atmosphere, ritual and time spent together are more important than the number of presents under the tree.'

Reena also recommends a 'magical' Danish holiday tradition, which involves holding hands round the Christmas tree after dinner, while you sing festive songs. 'Traditionally, this happens on the 23 December which is called "Little Christmas Eve",' she explains. '*Hygge* is never stronger than at Christmas. It's found in those shared moments that feel both ordinary and extraordinary, sipping *glogg* or mulled wine by candlelight, wrapping gifts while the fire glows, or playing games around the table after dinner.'

## 'Make it sustainable

Christmas is also the perfect time to channel the Scandinavian concept of *miljövänlighet*, which literally means "environmental friendliness" in Swedish. It's no accident that this outdoor-loving design aesthetic is also deeply entwined with sustainability and, when it comes to gifting, the Scandi approach is all about thoughtfulness and longevity.

Instead of throwaway or novelty trinkets, choose presents that are made to last, and are crafted from natural or recycled materials. Think hand-carved wooden toys, woollen scarves, organic candles or simple ceramics – items that are both beautiful and useful. When you're deciding whether to buy a product, take a moment to think about how it's packaged, too. We generate an estimated 125,000 tons of plastic packaging waste over Christmas in the UK alone, and a huge percentage of this winds up in landfill. By keeping gifts practical, well-made and low impact, you'll be embracing the Scandinavian ethos of sustainability while creating traditions that feel every bit as special.

When it comes to wrapping, opting for a Scandi look can make a big difference to our impact on the planet. Swap shiny or sparkly paper and plastic ribbons (which often aren't recyclable) for kraft paper, fabric offcuts or reusable linen bags. Ditch plastic-based tape, too, and seek out biodegradable alternatives, like Sellotape Zero Plastic, which is made from plant-based ingredients. Or opt for some simple cotton twine to neatly tie your gifts.

'Neutral, eco-friendly paper options will also complement the earthy tones of your tree,' adds Reena. 'Finish with a sprig of greenery, or make presents to loved ones extra special by adding mistletoe.'

Real Christmas trees are still the gold standard in Scandinavia, and they make an eco-friendly choice. Not only do they gobble carbon while they grow, they're also biodegradable and have a lower carbon footprint than fake ones shipped from abroad. To up your sustainability credentials further, plump for a potted tree, which you can re-plant in your garden and use year after year.

How to style Christmas the Scandi way

Decorate with evergreens and branches of berries

> "By stripping away the **EXCESS**, you create space for rituals that **MATTER**"

# Seasonal Scandi

Bring the outside in with this pared-back style that promotes seasonal wellness through mood-boosting greenery. Revel in Scandi-inspired simplicity with brass touches of luxury

## 'Peace and comfort

A luxe look in a living room calms the soul, especially when there's a touch of timber to bring a country vibe. Dress the tree with simple white decorations and wrap with warm fairy lights.

**BUY THE KEY PIECES**
Walls in Down Pipe estate eggshell, Farrow & Ball. Costello two and a half seater sofa in Olive velvet; Taylor coffee table, both Sofa.com. Baubles, from a selection at Cox & Cox

## Seasonal Scandi

**STYLE TIP**
Artificial sprays and sprigs of greenery work just as well as fresh and will still provide a botanical feel.

### Warm welcome
Ensure every space is dressed for the season, not forgetting the stairs. Wind lengths of laurel, ivy and sprigs of fir along the bannister and finish with simple paper stars.

**BUY THE KEY PIECES**
Clockhouse console table; large ribbed vase; Hoxton dome floor lamp, all Garden Trading

## Seasonal Scandi

### 'Delightful details

Trigger festive spirit with scented offerings. Easily home-crafted herb and spice firelighters will fill the air with seasonal fragrance.

**BUY THE KEY PIECES**
Lulworth side plate in Grey, Neptune

> "Have a go at **MAKING YOUR OWN WREATH** of greenery, using a halo of florist's foam peppered with off-cuts of fir, eucalyptus, holly and rosemary"

### 'Nature's best

Gather greenery into beautiful arrangements.

**BUY THE KEY PIECES**
Handmade wreath, Bird Studio. Glass vases, from a selection, LSA International

### Stylish setting

Keep things simple and dress the table with potted herbs.

**BUY THE KEY PIECES**
Luxury crackers, Nancy & Betty. Antonia napkins in Olive; Handsworth 24-piece cutlery set in Olive, both Neptune

**STYLE TIP**
Make firelighters by lining a muffin tin with paper cases, add melted soy wax, dried flowers and herbs, then leave to set.

## Take a seat

Create a chic dining setting by laying the table with considered crockery and glassware, interspersed with draped and potted festive foliage, buds and sprigs.

**BUY THE KEY PIECES**
Antonia napkins in Olive; Handsworth 24-piece cutlery set in Olive; Lulworth side plates in Grey, all Neptune. Luxury Christmas crackers; presents in Oak Leaves & Acorns wrapping paper, all Nancy & Betty

'Winter wonderland

# Winter wonderland

**Take your Scandi festivities up a notch with a Christmas trip to the Nordics**

Scandinavia is a very special part of the world. It is rich with history, a beguiling shared culture, otherworldly landscapes and fascinating traditions. Summer visitors will enjoy a fantastic stay, but Scandinavia saves much of its real wonder for the winter months. As streets glisten with frost and the sky comes alive with colour, the Nordics take on a magical quality. This magic is sometimes ethereal and atmospheric, like the pristine stillness of a jaw-dropping fjord, and sometimes it is charming and gleeful, like the welcoming hot cup of spiced *glogg*.

As you journey through Scandinavia you will encounter contrasts between the different countries and cultures, but you will also notice many similarities. This is thanks to their shared history, forged by centuries of trade and cultural exchange. Scandinavian countries each have their own national identities, but their close relationship means there is a shared cultural foundation – even the various languages are largely comprehensible to one another. You'll note similar cuisines (prepare to say "*hei!*" to lots of fish), a shared deep respect for the natural world, sleek designs and the warm pragmatism of Scandinavia's residents.

Chief among these values is a widespread love for the festive season. Winters here may be extremely cold, but you'll still feel warmed by the twinkling cosy atmosphere as Scandinavians settle in for their favourite time of year. Across the region, you'll experience *hygge*: a Swedish word for the feeling of cosiness, conviviality and warmth, enjoyed at a slower pace and centred around reveling in good times with loved ones. Indeed, a love for *hygge* will be your most valuable souvenir from your trip.

There are practical considerations to consider. Winter in the Nordics lasts from early November until the beginning of March. These months are especially cold (what else would you expect from a country called "Iceland"!), so be prepared to wrap up warm in layers and layers of clothes as temperatures drop below freezing, even in major cities. The number of daylight hours are minimal when you're this far north, so prepare yourself for hanging out in the dark.

Be sure to plan your trip finances carefully: this is a pricey part of the world. To stretch your budget, you could opt for self-catering accommodation, explore alternative options like hostels and apartments, use the region's public transport systems, and investigate discounts like Norway's Oslo Pass for cheaper entry into attractions. Saving in these ways means you can focus your splashing out on major adventures, like expert-led guided tours, world-famous fine dining or unique hotel experiences. However you plan to spend it, remember that each country here does have its own currency. Card payments (particularly contactless payments) are widely accepted.

Time your trip wisely to get the most out of differing local traditions. Winter here is a popular time for tourism, particularly for festive-themed activities like visiting Santa or shopping at the Christmas markets. There are also annual festivals to enjoy, such as Santa Lucia (celebrated by many Scandinavians on 13 December), or the festive finale of Saint Knut's Day, which takes place on 13 January in Sweden and Finland.

> **Scandinavia saves much of its real WONDER for the winter months**

Norway's Lofoten archipelago features dramatic mountain scenery

# Norway

Norway enjoys *friluftsliv*, roughly translating as "open-air living", all year round with a deep-rooted connection to the natural world. With such wonderful landscapes, it's no wonder the concept of disconnecting from daily stresses and spending time outdoors is so cherished.

Norway is the unofficial home of northern lights tours. Tromsø in the north is the launchpad for many a lights show, earning the nickname "gateway to the Arctic". Of course, the aurora borealis can be spotted across many places in Scandinavia, but Tromsø is certainly one of the most famous. Your best chances of viewing this mesmerising phenomenon are during Tromsø's longest nights from late November to mid-January. This is when you can experience Polar Night, the days where the sun never truly rises.

Back on the ground, Norwegians find many inventive ways to enjoy winter. Skiing is popular here, both downhill and cross country. Go hiking through epic landscapes, like the famed Pulpit Rock, or let the dogs do the miles for you and go sledding with huskies across Finnmark.

Take to the water and experience the country's stunning fjords. There are over a thousand fjords lining the Norwegian coastline. UNESCO declared the West Norwegian Fjords – Geirangerfjord and Nærøyfjord – as World Heritage Sites in honour of their sheer scale and beauty, making nearby Bergen the go-to city for fjord-hopping. Indeed, travelling to and from the charming Bergen is itself a spectacular activity: take an unforgettable train ride on the renowned Flåm Railway.

Once you've got your fill of fresh air, it's time to enjoy some *kos*, the Norwegian twist on Scandinavia's *hygge*. Cosiness, simple pleasures and time well spent are central to Norway's winters: enjoy hot drinks, gingerbreads and hearty stews as you hear about the rich culture of folklore and tales of their Viking heritage.

If your visit is a festive one, take part in the wide-ranging Christmas traditions. Join in by sipping a seasonal beer (*Juleøl*) at a lively party (*Julebord*) in the run up to Christmas, or decorating trees with paper lanterns and eating rice puddings on 23 December (*Lille Julaften*, or "Little Christmas Eve").

## TRAVELLER TIPS

**TIMEZONE** CET / CEST
**CURRENCY** Norwegian Krone
**LANGUAGE** Norwegian, English is widespread
**EMERGENCY NUMBER** 110 for fire services, 112 for police, 113 for ambulance
**TYPICAL WINTER CLIMATE** In Oslo: -5 to +5°C in Tromsø: -6 to +2°C

# Denmark

Denmark is a stylish stop on your trip through Scandinavia. Danish culture is rich and founded in a sumptuous history, including the legendary Vikings, one of the earliest European royal families and a long string of important authors, philosophers, artists and scientists. Denmark wears its storied history well: the capital city of Copenhagen is a beautiful waterside spot with pretty cobbled streets, colourful houses, decadent palaces and plenty of that famous Scandi style.

Danish Christmas is celebrated on the 24 December, with *Julemanden* (the local version of Santa) delivering presents to children. In Danish tradition, elves (or "*nisse*"), assist *Julemanden* on his mission, so be sure to keep an eye out for these mythical creatures.

One of Scandinavia's most famous Christmas markets happens in Tivoli Gardens, the traditional amusement park in the heart of Copenhagen, running from mid-November until the early days of January every year. This renowned market features everything you can dream of for a truly magical market: snow-covered stalls, twinkling lights, and even festive-themed rides.

Outside of Tivoli Gardens, other Danish landmarks deck themselves out for a festive feel. Nyhavn, the iconic colourful canalside district, is the backdrop to one of the country's most photogenic Christmas markets. Beyond the traditional stalls, Nyhavn is home to delightful bars, restaurants, and shops. Explore the works of the founding father of fairytales: the Hans Christian Andersen museum is here.

Denmark is famous for having some of the world's most well-regarded restaurants. With careful planning, you could snag a table at Noma, the iconic multi-Michelin-star hotspot. If a reservation there proves too elusive, there are plenty of other exceptional menus across Denmark, all boasting serious accolades for their "New Nordic" cuisine. In between all your fine dining, pick through the food halls for *Smørrebrød*, open-faced rye-bread sandwiches topped with butters and local delicacies. Throughout winter this dish will take on a seasonal slant, with the popular topping *æbleflæsk* (apple pork).

Perhaps once you've toured the canals, markets and restaurants of Denmark, you can take part in another beloved Danish tradition: the winter swim! Harbours are popular spots for an ice-cold plunge: Copenhagen, Aarhus and Odense are major hubs for icy dips. There's a winter wild swimming festival on the stunning Danish island of Langeland in February, and increasing numbers of Danes are found jumping into the waters as an emerging New Year's Day tradition.

Nyhavn is the waterfront heart of capital Copenhagen

## TRAVELLER TIPS

**TIMEZONE** CET / CEST
**CURRENCY** Danish Krone
**LANGUAGE** Danish, English is widespread
**EMERGENCY NUMBER** 112
**TYPICAL WINTER CLIMATE** In Copenhagen: -1 to +8°C, with snow, wind and rain

'Winter wonderland

# Sweden

Sweden, the largest country in Scandinavia, offers a mix of stylish city breaks, charming traditions and adrenaline-pumping adventures. Come winter, the whole country is often blanketed in snow, giving a picturesque backdrop to your visit. However you choose to spend your Swedish trip, you will be embraced by the concept of *hygge*: cosiness, contentment, and conviviality.

The north is home to the indigenous Scandinavian people: the Sámi. Their ancient and storied history is today celebrated with continued traditions of reindeer herding, ice fishing and crafting. If you love wildlife, this is the place to seek out arctic animals like native moose, wolves and wild reindeer. Many of these beautiful experiences will begin in Kiruna, the hub for Sámi-led responsible tourism.

Kiruna, up in Swedish Lapland, is the best place to get your northern lights fix, thanks to its long, star-speckled nights. It's also the closest city to the famous ICEHOTEL, the world's first hotel made of ice. Each year, the rooms are built afresh with artists sculpting away in time for the winter season (there are also cosy log cabins if you get cold feet!). If you want to stay here, book in before the ice rooms melt back into the nearby rivers in April.

Skiing is a Swedish mainstay thanks to its dependable snow and excellent infrastructure. There are hundreds of resorts to choose from, with one of the most prominent ski towns being Åre. If you're up for a challenge, time your trip with Vasaloppet, the legendary cross country ski race which takes place on the first Sunday in March.

Sweden's capital Stockholm makes for a delightful city getaway. It's a prime spot to dabble in *fika* – the social ritual of taking a break with a cup of coffee and sweet treats.

Covered in snow throughout winter, Stockholm's charming old town, Gamla Stan, is a colourful island of cobbled streets and 17th-century architecture. It hosts Sweden's oldest Christmas market, with another popular event being the Skansen Christmas market held at the open-air museum and zoo. Market dates vary each year, so check dates before you travel, but most will be up and running from late November for Christmas shopping!

For even more of a festive fix, embrace some Swedish Christmas traditions. Experience a candlelit ceremony on Santa Lucia Day (13 December), get creative by building a *pepparkakshus* (gingerbread house), and enjoy a delicious *Julbord* feast on Christmas Eve.

Stockholm's picturesque Södermalm island

## TRAVELLER TIPS

**TIMEZONE** CET / CEST
**CURRENCY** Swedish Krona
**LANGUAGE** Swedish, English is widespread
**EMERGENCY NUMBER** 112
**TYPICAL WINTER CLIMATE**
In Stockholm: -4 to +6°C
In Kiruna: -17 to -2°C

'Winter wonderland

## Iceland

Possibly the most dramatic of all the Nordic landscapes, Iceland stands apart quite literally from its continental contemporaries. On the cusp of the North Atlantic and Arctic oceans, Iceland isn't technically a part of Scandinavia, but thanks to their previously Danish rule and a shared historical and cultural background, it is often grouped alongside its fellow Nordic nations.

It's a country defined by spectacular natural scenery: think explosive geysers, remote icy wilderness, vast volcanoes and shimmering glaciers. It has declared itself the "land of ice and fire", a fitting adage for this ancient land ruled by the elements. In winter, experience Iceland's extremes with additional impact: daylight hours are minimal and the arctic climate rolls through. Indoors, though, Icelanders are getting extra cosy with warming drinks and mischievous traditions.

Visitors in the Christmas period might meet the "Yule Lads", mysterious mythical characters who, when provided with an offering of shoes or bread, leave you a gift. Any children joining your trip should be mindful of two Icelandic figures: Gryla, the ogre mother of the Yule Lads who eats naughty children, and her pet the Yule Cat, who eats anyone who doesn't get new clothes before Christmas Eve. Join the annual hunt across Reykjavík to see if you can find all the festive creatures from Icelandic folklore.

Warmed by the Icelandic sense of humour, head outdoors to experience this extraordinary landscape. The island is home to incredible natural phenomena which has to be seen to be believed. Take unforgettable walks through the Geysir Geothermal Area, head on hikes across glaciers or explore the depths of ice caves. Choose expert-led tours for optimal safety and enjoyment.

To relax, take a dip in the world-famous geothermal waters of the Blue Lagoon. Winter is also the prime time to see the northern lights, so head out away from the city for a dedicated tour, or stay overnight in special glass igloos.

A winter trip to Iceland is an ideal opportunity to view the northern lights

### TRAVELLER TIPS

**TIMEZONE** GMT
**CURRENCY** Icelandic Króna
**LANGUAGE** Icelandic, English is widespread
**EMERGENCY NUMBER** 112
**TYPICAL WINTER CLIMATE** In Reykjavík: -2 to +5°C, with snow

Visit the stunning snow-covered landscapes of Lapland

> **TRAVELLER TIPS**
>
> **TIMEZONE** EET / EEST
> **CURRENCY** Euro
> **LANGUAGE** Finnish, English is widespread
> **EMERGENCY NUMBER** 112
> **TYPICAL WINTER CLIMATE**
> In Helsinki: -7 to +5°C
> In Rovaniemi: -14 to -2°C

# Finland

While Finland isn't technically part of Scandinavia, it is a part of the Nordics and shares many customs and cultural touchpoints with its neighbours. Many wintertime visitors will choose to focus their Finnish plans in the north, closer to the Arctic Circle for maximum frost. Indeed, Finland is almost synonymous with Lapland, the country's northernmost region.

Lapland is, of course, the hometown of the world's most famous gift-giver: Father Christmas. The Finnish claim the legend originates from Rovaniemi, a picturesque city nestled in spectacular surroundings. The city is small enough to explore on foot: be sure to delve into the indigenous Sámi culture at the stunning Arktikum museum and sample local delicacies (roasted reindeer, anyone?) before heading out to explore the nearby Santa Claus Village.

Santa Claus Village is the ultimate festive trip. Open year round, this is where you'll meet Finland's most famed resident. The Village itself offers a wide range of themed activities, from a visit to Santa's post office to daily meet-and-greets with the main man himself. Browse for gifts at the workshops, pet Santa's trusty reindeers, and take a crash course in elf skills at the Elf Academy.

Lapland also has its fair share of snow-fuelled adventures. Adrenaline-seeking takes on a snowy twist here, as you can explore the spectacular scenery on a snowmobile, or even with the help of a crew of huskies! Dog sledding is perhaps the most exciting form of transport in the area, and certainly the cutest.

Whether you've spent the day revelling in festive cheer or thrill-seeking, you can reset with a traditional Finnish sauna. This steamy tradition is enjoyed year-round, but takes on a new revitalising quality in the depths of winter. Saunas are intrinsic to Finnish culture, with reportedly upwards of 3 million saunas in the country. The snow sauna in the Arctic SnowHotel is a popular spot, or head to the "sauna capital of the world", Tampere, which boasts Finland's oldest public sauna.

# Good tidings

Serendipity played a part in Alex and Chelsea being able to build this gorgeous home from scratch – it's a dream come true

### Dining area

Chelsea usually forages in the nearby woodlands for leaves and twigs to make a wreath like this to sit above the Christmas table. The built-in bleached oak seating and shelves offer practical storage and add character to the house.

**BUY THE KEY PIECES**
Walls in Raw White, Bauwerk Colour. Handmade wreath, Larkspur & Lavender. Vintage Spanish chair covered in Mont Blanc leather from Moore & Giles. Tablecloth, Zara Home. Green candleholders and green baubles, Gisela Graham. Pale brown glass candleholders; twisted candles; candy ornaments, all Broste Copenhagen. Marbled bowl, Henry Holland. Brown and cream patterned baubles and striped baubles, all Rowen & Wren. Murano swirl glasses, The Edition 94. Light, Nelson Wright Architects

## Kitchen

A mix of materials gives a vintage vibe – bleached oak cupboards, steel door fronts and marble surfaces – a long way from the kitchen fit-out in your average new build.

**BUY THE KEY PIECES**
Similar 1960s Italian pendants by Tommaso Barbi and vintage downlights, Thurstan. Custom kitchen, Nelson Wright Architects; worktops in Calacatta Michelangelo marble, Middlesex Marble. Bar stools, Frama. Similar metal candelabra, Etsy. Glasses, Broste Copenhagen. Metal wreath, Curated Living

### Living room

'I designed pocket doors so the space between the living room and kitchen can be used open plan or closed off for more intimacy,' says Alex. The courtyard garden beyond has cooking and seating areas so the couple hang out there a lot.

**BUY THE KEY PIECES**
Engineered oak flooring, Havwoods. Wall-mounted light, Nelson Wright Architects. Vase (on shelf) by Jo Modern Potter at M.A.H gallery. Bowl (on shelf) by Joanna Ling at The Edition 94. Baubles (in bowl), Cox & Cox

# Good tidings

When you've just built a house, plus the one next door, established an architectural practice and, er, had a baby, life can be pretty full-on. So when it comes to the festive season, you deserve to put your feet up. 'We intend to,' says architect Alex Wright, one half, with interior designer partner Chelsea Nelson, of Nelson Wright Architects. 'My mum is Finnish so in Scandi style we celebrate with our big meal on Christmas Eve with close family who live nearby.' The next day, all of them, including baby Rufus, venture out for a nature walk in the ancient woodland forest minutes from their home in east London.

The couple's festive decorating style reflects their pared-back, millennial-hip, house vibe – 'just elevated with foraged branches, twigs, fir cones and candles to dress it up a bit,' explains Alex.

Life does feel rather surreal for Alex and Chelsea, who went from renting a flat to finding a piece of land, building two houses – they were aiming for one but serendipitously a plot next door became available, so it made sense to build two – to living in their own bespoke home, all within a few years. 'It is quite the dream,' says Alex.

Before establishing their own practice, Alex specialised in residential work for architectural firms and Chelsea was an interior designer at Soho House. The second of the homes they built was sold as soon as it was finished, a sigh of relief for the couple, who had been funding the project, with Alex's mother as a guarantor. Each house enjoys the same contemporary take on the Victorian stock in the vicinity, earning approval of both the planners and, more importantly, the neighbours. 'Crucial when you are living amongst them,' explains Alex.

Creating their home was very much a joint enterprise, says Alex. 'I focused on the strategic stuff and technical design, Chelsea's approach was more conceptual.'

His warm minimalist perspective is enhanced by Chelsea's layered and expressive off-white neutral tones, heavy textures and tactile materials. Her 3D visual boards helped the couple firm up decisions on furniture – mainly bespoke or vintage – and on their use of characterful natural materials – wood, steel, marble and brass. Alex is rightly proud of its standout features, such as the exposed ceiling rafters, a triple-height sculptural staircase topped with a roof skylight, and its eco-credentials, which mean it's very economical to run.

Despite the challenges of juggling finances and lockdown which came at the beginning of the build, the couple describe the 14-month-long project, completed in 2021, as 'fun and a true labour of love'. 'And doing it for yourself means you have that freedom to just please yourself,' concludes Alex.

Having had such a good experience, they mean to carry on, with plans to expand their residential portfolio by developing a small block of flats in south London. Certainly never a dull moment.

## HOME NOTES

### WHO LIVES HERE?
Architect Alex Wright and his partner Chelsea Nelson, an interior designer, plus their baby son Rufus. Together they designed and built two side-by-side houses that led them to establish their own practice, Nelson Wright Architects (**nelson-wright.com**).

### THE PROPERTY
A contemporary-meets-Victorian new build in east London. On the ground floor are the living, dining and kitchen areas, plus a cloakroom. The first floor has the main bedroom and a bathroom, Rufus' room and a utility. The second floor has a spare bedroom, office and wet room, plus sauna-cum-bathroom.

Good tidings

### Living room

'The sofa was custom made in a traditional way in Portugal; it's super comfy and durable, which is important with an infant in the house,' says Chelsea.

**BUY THE KEY PIECES**
Sofa, Chelsea Upholstery & Interiors. Cushions, H&M Home and made in fabric by Le Manach. Vintage brass artwork, Thurstan. Asata brass candleholders, Ligne Roset. Marbled bowl, Henry Holland. Baubles in bowl: Curious Egg, Broste Copenhagen, Cox & Cox. Wrapping paper: Curated living, Rowen & Wren, Nancy & Betty

'Living room

Exposed ceiling rafters here and in almost all the spaces bring a wonderful sense of character to the home.

**BUY THE KEY PIECES**
Chair and ottoman, both Chelsea Upholstery & Interiors. Try 1stDibs for a similar 1950s French teak bench and 1960s French glass grape chandelier. Throw, The British Blanket Company. Curtains in a Volga Linen fabric. Similar vintage floor lamp, Vinterior. Rug, London House Rugs

## Office

The couple both work from this space at the top of the house. It is multifunctional and is also used as a yoga studio and spare bedroom.

**BUY THE KEY PIECES**
Walls in Off-White, Farrow & Ball. Desk/shelving system, Atelier Belge. Flooring, Havwoods. Similar white vintage chair, Pamono. 1930s Fritz Hansen wooden chair and brass 1980s Italian desk lamp, both Vinterior. Rug, Moore & Giles. White 1950s French clip-on lamp, Etsy

### Main bathroom
Seen in the mirror is a glimpse of the double shower, which has a skylight above. 'You feel like you're outside in the elements, which is delightful whether sunny or rainy,' says Alex.

**BUY THE KEY PIECES**
Wall tiles, In Situ. Sink and taps, both Aston Matthews. Cabinetry, Nelson Wright Architects. Handles, Louis Fraser. Similar old barber's mirror, Etsy. Wall lights, Lamp Factory London

Good tidings

### Bathroom
As a Finn, Alex couldn't live without a wet room (which adjoins this space) and a sauna. Wooden slats pull down over the bath so it can be used as a sauna.
**BUY THE KEY PIECES**
Bath, Aston Matthews. Bespoke sauna, Nelson Wright Architects

### Study space
Alex designed an atrium to flood light all the way down the staircase to the bottom of the house. A mini desk area was created as a quiet place to read or work.
**BUY THE KEY PIECES**
Desk, Nelson Wright Architects. 1930s wooden chair by Fritz Hansen, Vinterior. 1950s French desk light, Thurstan

> Simple, stripped-back architectural expression is contrasted with handmade and artisanal materials, which develop patina and signs of use over time, **CELEBRATING IMPERFECTIONS**

30
SCANDI CHRISTMAS

### Main bedroom

Keeping the rafters exposed provides extra ceiling height.

**BUY THE KEY PIECES**
Ceiling in Pointing, Farrow & Ball. Bed, Thurstan. Ceiling light, Nelson Wright Architects. Throw, The British Blanket Company. Similar bedside table, Vinterior. Artwork by Filipa Tojal. Lamp, Collier Webb

# Alternative Advent

Create an extra special lead-up to the festivities by making your own unique handcrafted Advent calendar, and let the countdown to Christmas begin

### Upcycle toilet roll tubes

**Bring a little festive cheer with a Scandi-inspired Advent calendar.**

You will need 24 cardboard tubes all the same size.

Use number stickers to secure one end of each of your tubes. If your stickers are smaller than the end of the tube, cut tissue paper circles that are 1.5cm (¾") larger in diameter than your tube and use glue to cover one end of each tube, then stick on your numbers.

Randomly place the tubes inside wooden triangular frames.

Fill the tubes from the reverse with little gifts and treats, then stuff the end with tissue paper.

**BUY THE KEY PIECES**
Cardboard craft tubes; wooden triangular frames, all Hobbycraft. Advent stickers; Folklore glass baubles, all The Danes. Glitter stars, Meri Meri. Pom-pom garland, find similar at Notonthehighstreet.com

# Alternative Advent

**BUY THE KEY PIECES**
Straight couplers, B&Q. Papers; patterned birch decorative stars, all Cambridge Imprint. String, from a selection, The Danes

**STYLE TIP**
You can tie the copper tubes in place with off-cuts of felt or fabric too.

## 'Make a copper tubing mobile

**Simple and understated, these hanging scrolls add a stylish touch to a bare wall.**

Cut a piece of copper pipe into 24 2.5cm (1") pieces (or use copper pipe couplers).

Use a white marker pen to write the numbers 1-24 on the pipe pieces.

Tie a length of string to each pipe.

Take a wooden dowel and tie the pipe pieces below at differing heights in a random numerical order.

Cut 24 pieces of decorative paper, around 7x5cm (2¾x2"). On the reverse of each, write a daily activity. Roll up and thread each one through a piece of pipe.

Tie a length of string at each end of the wooden dowel, add a few decorations and hang in place.

## Alternative Advent

### Fill glass jars with wrapped sweets

A little treat every morning, for adults and children alike.

Select jars large enough for 24 sweets. Remove the lids and spray-paint them in your chosen colour.

Use hot glue to attach a festive decoration.

Once dry, spray the lid again so the decoration blends seamlessly. Add Christmas tattoo transfers for an extra festive finish to the glass of the jars.

Put numbered stickers on your treats and fill the jars.

**STYLE TIP**
Swap out animal toppers for a painted wooden initial, covered in glitter.

**BUY THE KEY PIECES**
Vintage-style Mason jar, Amazon. Clear jar; spray paint and ribbon, from a selection, all Hobbycraft. Christmas tattoos, Meri Meri

SCANDI CHRISTMAS

### Peg paper bags onto a simple memo board

**If you've left things a little last minute then this idea is super-quick to make.**

Fill 24 little bags with treats.

Fold over the tops of the bags, secure with a sticker and number the bags 1-24.

If you wish to add decorations to the bags you can attach stickers, wooden craft pieces or washi tape.

Use mini bulldog clips to attach to a memo board.

**BUY THE KEY PIECES**
Memo boards, Poundland. Gold bulldog clips, Amazon. Block bottom Kraft bags; block bottom Ivory bags; Nordic woodland stickers, all The Danes. Wooden house embellishments; small Black number stickers, all Hobbycraft. Rectangular border stickers, Cambridge Imprint

**STYLE TIP**
Peg the bags to ribbon instead, to hang from a fireplace or dado rail.

## Attach an envelope Advent tree

Minimal effort and maximum impact, arrange numbered envelopes in varying sizes to create a Christmas tree shape on the wall.

Select 23 envelopes of varying colours and sizes. Use adhesive numbers to randomly number the envelopes 1-23.

Place cards within the envelopes that can either give clues to hunt out Advent gifts; positive affirmations; special activities or treats.

Lay the envelopes out to work out your design. When happy with the layout use Blu Tack to stick the envelopes in place on the wall.

Finish with a star numbered 24.

### STYLE TIP
Use envelopes that match your Christmas theme, choosing different shades for interest.

**BUY THE KEY PIECES**
Plain envelopes, from a selection; gold adhesive numbers; paper ball on floor, all Hobbycraft. Snowflake envelopes; Crimson patterned envelopes; folk decorations; gift wraps, from a selection, all Cambridge Imprint. Paper balls on mantel, from a selection at Meri Meri. Mini Folklore baubles, The Danes

# Alternative Advent

## 'Bunch up foliage as a showstopping advent topper

### HOW TO WAX SEAL

Ring in the season with a natural touch by hanging a swathe of foliage above pretty wax sealed envelopes hung on string.

### YOU WILL NEED
- Cards, envelopes and pen
- Ribbon and string
- Double-sided tape
- Wax and wax seal stamp
- Selection of foliage
- 85cm (2'10") rope or sash cord
- Length of metal wire

**BUY THE KEY PIECES**
Mini gift card envelopes, Amazon. Ribbon; Gold seal wax; heart seal wax stamp; mixed gold number stickers, all Hobbycraft

### STEP 1
Place a little card in each envelope with an Advent daily activity written on each. Cut a length of ribbon long enough to wrap around the centre of the envelope. Secure in place with double-sided tape.

### STEP 2
Melt wax to cover the join in the ribbon; while hot push the stamp into the wax. Turn envelope over and attach string for hanging. Repeat with all 24 envelopes.

### STEP 3
Use the wire to tie bunches of foliage along the length of the rope. Tie a length of string around 15cm in from one end and 30cm in from the other end to hang.

### STEP 4
Stick adhesive numbers from 1-24 to the front of the envelopes. Finish by tying the decorated envelopes onto the foliage swag at varying heights.

FEATURE AND STYLING MARIE NICHOLS PHOTOGRAPHS DAN DUCHARS

# IT'S TIME TO
# Embrace the cold

**Forget doom and gloom, we reveal the latest wellbeing trend for making the most of winter**

The clocks have gone back, we've cranked up the central heating, and now the long, wintry months stretch out ahead. But there's no need to dread colder, darker days – in fact, there are plenty of reasons in which this season boosts wellbeing. Not only has it been proven that cold weather can be beneficial for our health, but the quieter, slower months are a chance to restore and heal. Here's the lowdown on why it's time to welcome winter.

## THE BENEFITS OF A BIT OF BRRRR

What do you want to do when the temperature plummets? Snuggle up under a blanket with a hot chocolate in front of the TV? You could be missing a trick – if you want to ease your aches and pains, feel happier, sleep more soundly and even stave off dementia, you might want to get up and get out.

### Head outdoors

Aim for every day – even just for a walk. Any exercise outside can help to prevent circulatory disease, cancer, diabetes, obesity, depression and other serious conditions, explains Dr Melanie Wynne-Jones, but doing it in cold weather brings further benefits. The elements make your body work harder than when exercising indoors. Plus, the cold triggers your body's brown fat (a type of fat that helps to maintain your body temperature when you get too cold) to burn more calories.

### Go wild in water

Open-air swimming is so popular it's practically mainstream now, and it seems that Brits are not put off by bad weather. More than 4.1 million people regularly take a dip in England's seas, lakes and rivers, according to Sport England. Wellbeing experts believe this can supercharge health. There's evidence that an outdoor dip is good for the nervous system, and it will provide you with a rush of feel-good endorphins. But it is important to note that extremes of temperature should be avoided by those with high blood pressure, heart conditions or asthma, and by pregnant women.

### Try to adopt a Scandi mindset

Our ability to cope with harsh winters could be down to outlook alone. In a town on the Norwegian coast – 200 miles north of the Arctic Circle – the sun doesn't rise above the horizon, and temperatures drop well below freezing, for months. Despite these bleak conditions, researchers found that locals don't dread the darkness or have low moods. Instead, they thrive due to a "positive winter mindset", which sees them enjoying cold-weather activities such as skiing or polar hiking, and celebrating *koselig*, which means a sense of cosiness.

### Have a *friluftsliv* winter

This Nordic concept roughly translates to "open-air living" and Brits can get on board by following the Norwegian mantra of "there's no such thing as bad weather, only bad clothes". Wrap up well to do a minimum of 150 minutes of physical activity outside each week. Nature will boost feelings of wellbeing, so switch off your phone and soak up the seasonal surroundings.

## RISE AND SHINE!

**Wake up happier on those dark and chilly mornings**

### FAKE NATURAL LIGHT
Invest in an alarm clock that recreates sunlight to gradually wake you slowly and naturally. Try Lumie Sunrise Alarm (**lumie.com**).

### STRETCH IT OUT
Gentle morning stretches will wake up your muscles, boost circulation, stimulate your digestive system and reduce feelings of stress.

### FUEL YOURSELF
A high-protein breakfast such as salmon and eggs will kick-start the day and keep your energy levels high throughout the morning.

## A LITTLE WINTER WEIGHT GAIN

While being overweight may lead to health problems, carrying a few extra pounds when it's cold can have benefits. 'Fat is hugely important. It only gets a bad rep when the body stores too much,' says fitness expert and nutritionist Yvonne Wake. (wellbeingandlifestyle.co.uk) 'Fat is what keeps us warm when the weather is freezing, and we get our energy from our fat stores. It also protects the body from trauma by acting as a physical cushion.'

So don't feel guilty about increased portion sizes of hearty, comforting meals, just be sure to keep your body mass index (BMI) between 18.5 and 24.9, to stay healthy. Use the BMI calculator at **nhs.uk**.

## The power of hibernation

Do shorter days make you sleepier? Darkness triggers the release of the sleep hormone melatonin, and during the winter we should adapt our lifestyle and rest patterns to accommodate its increase. Plus, hunkering down for more kip is not such a bad thing. Going into reboot mode helps bodily processes – from circulation, digestion and stress regulation to tissue healing and muscle growth.

'Recuperative sleep is one of the most important restorative mechanisms available to humans, allowing for recovery from daily stresses and strains, and is essential for daily functioning and health,' says Mark Cropley, professor of health psychology at the University of Surrey.

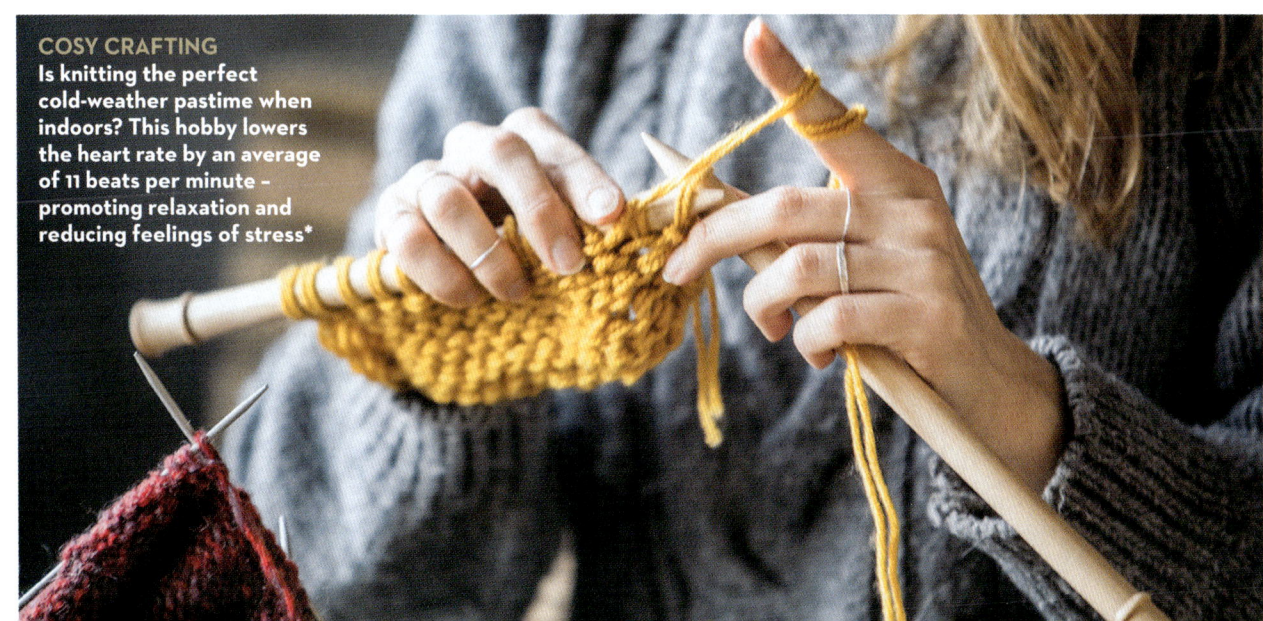

**COSY CRAFTING**
Is knitting the perfect cold-weather pastime when indoors? This hobby lowers the heart rate by an average of 11 beats per minute – promoting relaxation and reducing feelings of stress*

# Festive flair

Christmas is a modern affair in Katie Seidler's family home with the decorations chiming with the Scandi-influenced decor

### Dining area

The slimline tree is perfect for popping behind the dining table, out of the way but still in view from the living area.

**BUY THE KEY PIECES**
Pre-lit Norway Spruce Christmas tree, Balsam Hill. Table, Made by Wood. Chairs, Takt. Artwork, The Poster Club. Similar natural ribbon pendant lights, John Lewis & Partners

# 'Festive flair

### Kitchen

'I love open shelving in the kitchen as I believe this space doesn't have to be purely functional,' says Katie. 'I can display my favourite ceramics and plants alongside useful items such as coffee pots and cookbooks.'

**BUY THE KEY PIECES**
Shelves, Ikea. Similar hanging star decoration, Layered Lounge

### Study space

Part of the kitchen has been painted in a sandy colour to bring warmth to the space, while a small wood table provides an additional dining spot.

**BUY THE KEY PIECES**
Walls in Packed Sand, Valspar. Dining table and chairs, Takt. Plant pot, Made. Under the Bell pendant light, Muuto

## HOME NOTES

### WHO LIVES HERE?
Katie Seidler, owner of interior design studio **@hello_haus**, with her husband Russell and their French bulldog, Henry.

### THE PROPERTY
A detached three-bed Victorian home in St Albans.

## 'Living area

This is part of the open-plan space, with a door to the kitchen on the left and the dining area to the right. 'Whoever is in the living area is near enough to the kitchen that we can still chat to each other,' says Katie.

**BUY THE KEY PIECES**
Sofa, Made. Coffee table, Bloomingville. Armchair; log holder, both Ikea. Lamp base, H&M Home. Lamp shade, Ferm Living. Rug, Nordic Knots. Artwork, Studio Paradissi. Similar floorstanding paper Christmas trees, Layered Lounge.

Christmas is all about family in the Seidler household. The big day is spent with loved ones, the lead-up is full of cosy nights at home with a glass of red wine and a mince pie or two in front of the wood burner. However, Katie, whose Victorian house is in a busy market town in Hertfordshire, will admit that she likes to keep the decorations simple and minimal, with lots of natural elements that fit in with their home's pared-back Scandi style.

Having bought the three-bedroom property, after many years of renting, Katie and her husband Russell were keen to make their mark on the place and fill it with their love of Scandinavian design. 'Although the house didn't need any structural work, the interior was very plain and hadn't been used to its full potential at all,' says Katie. 'I could instantly see how we could transform it to make it work for us.'

With no major work to be done, painting was carried out and a new wood floor installed. Katie wanted to ensure the house was cohesive, light and serene, and describes her vision as a mix of 'Japanese style and Scandi design'. Her love of Danish furniture, clean lines

*Festive flair*

> "By changing to an open-plan layout we've achieved a light, **UNCLUTTERED** space that feels warm and homely"

### Landing

The calming, neutral tones continue upstairs, where the banister is also used to arrange some festive decorations.

**BUY THE KEY PIECES**
Shelf unit, Wayfair.
Print, Made

# Festive flair

### Bathroom
Pale colours have been used in the bathroom as a backdrop for artwork, plants and accessories. 'By using paint effectively and changing up the small accessories and little details, you can totally transform a space,' says Katie.

**BUY THE KEY PIECES**
Mirror, shelf and hooks, Gejst Design

### Bedroom
The muted palette continues in here with a warm beige wall framing the bed beautifully.

**BUY THE KEY PIECES**
Walls in Packed Sand, Valspar. Penn bed, Made. Pendant light, Crea-Re Studio. Bedspread, Ferm Living. Artwork, The Poster Club

### Office space
'The loft room was where we tried to fit three goals into one room,' says Katie. 'It needed to be a spare bedroom, have storage space and include a home office for me. It's probably one of the most practical rooms in the house.'

**BUY THE KEY PIECES**
Walls in Parchment, Craig & Rose. Desk, Tiptoe. Chair, Ikea. Lamp, HomeSense

'A smart space-saving idea was to use two shelves as bedside tables they look SLEEK AND STYLISH'

and lots of texture were the focus when designing each room, with her eye for detail ensuring every corner and nook has been well planned.

The Seidlers' living and dining space was previously used as one large living area, but Katie quickly turned it into a more functional room where they could entertain as well as relax. 'Zoning is key,' she says, 'I've used rugs to turn the two areas into distinct spaces. Everyone needs their home to work for them and I think we need to ensure it's how we want to live right now and not necessarily worry about future owners.'

The biggest job the couple had to contend with was the kitchen, where they ripped out the old worktops and took off wall cabinets to open up the space. The worktops were replaced, the walls were tiled and a new sink, hob and wall shelves added.

Nowhere does Katie's love of natural materials and wood come into play more than in the home office, where wooden batons were installed onto the wall for a slatted effect. They add a warmth to the room that's calm and subtle, while adding impact, albeit in a more natural form. Keeping to the same colours in each room also means they flow from one to the other seamlessly and enables Katie to move furniture and accessories around easily, as they work in every space. 'Danish brands are my go-to when it comes to furniture and accessories; Ferm Living, Hay, Normann Copenhagen and Takt, for example,' she says.

With the interior complete, the Seidlers were able to turn their attention to the exterior, where they gave their compact garden a neat refresh. They employed the help of a local company, who landscaped it and built planters around the edge, which took around a month. 'I'd love a bigger garden so I could build my dream garden office, but we've made the best use of the small space,' she says.

Asked about her finishing touches, Katie confirms that she still has a huge list to go. She's constantly tweaking the small things and helping the house evolve. 'I'm not the most patient person and there's been so much I've wanted to change but it takes time,' she says. 'Creating a home you love can be a slow process. I'm so pleased with what we've achieved, though, and I'm looking forward to showing off our hard work at Christmas.'

# Card tricks

Want to make Christmas that little bit extra special? Then look no further than our simple ideas for one-of-a-kind cards

### 3D paper bauble

**Create a simple single bauble or you can make a little cluster for extra impact.**

Use a craft punch to cut eight paper circles from decorative paper.

Fold each circle in half and create a central crease.

Place the circles on top of each other – decorative side up and with central creases aligned. Hold in place on one side with a paper clip.

Use cotton and thread to stitch together along the central crease. Then remove the paper clip.

Turn over the stitched circles, apply glue to the reverse of the bottom circle and place into position on your card. Then fan out each 'leaf' of the sphere to create a 3D bauble shape.

Finish with a bow and a couple of stick-on gems. Christmas Kraft tape adds the final festive touch.

**BUY THE KEY PIECES**
Natural card and envelope; DMC Gold light effects embroidery thread; adhesive pearl strips, all Hobbycraft. Christmas Kraft tape, The Danes. Papers, The Cambridge Imprint

# Card tricks

**BUY THE KEY PIECES**
Dark Green cards; Natural cards; ribbon from a selection, all Hobbycraft. Glitter stars, Meri Meri. Baubles, from a selection, Garden Trading. Mirror and candlestick, Weathered & Worn

## Twig trees

Nature-inspired twig and ribbon trees that are so simple to make the whole family can get involved.

Starting at the base of the twig, tie your off-cut of ribbon in place with a simple knot. Repeat the process up the length of the twig.

Trim the ends of the ribbons to create a tree shape. Use hot glue to attach the twig to the card and finish with a glitter star on top of the tree.

# Card tricks

**STYLE TIP**
To add colour to your card, tie a thin piece of ribbon in a bow at the top of the wreath.

### Hand-drawn Christmas door

A simple Kraft card and a Sharpie can create a striking design.

Use a pencil to sketch out your door design.

When you're happy go over the design using a black marker. Once the ink is dry, use a rubber to erase any visible pencil lines.

Use wooden foliage shapes and hot glue to create a wreath and attach to the 'door'.

**BUY THE KEY PIECES**
Natural cards; mini wooden vine leaf shapes; Black markers, all Hobbycraft. Marble cake stand, from a selection at H&M. Decorative bottle brush tree, The Danes

## Hand-stitched motifs

**Simple stitched designs using metallic thread will 'wow' their recipients.**

Choose a dark-coloured card to best show off the metallic thread.

Lightly pencil on your design.

Thread your needle with a length of metallic yarn, tying a knot at the end.

Starting on the reverse of the card push the needle through the card and start stitching your pattern.

Finish on the reverse with a knot and trim off any excess thread.

Add any stickers, ribbon or gem embellishments to finish.

**BUY THE KEY PIECES**
Gutermann metallic thread; Black cards and envelopes; Black square cards and envelopes; Gold adhesive gems; Gold Merry Christmas foil stickers, ribbon from a selection, all Hobbycraft

**STYLE TIP**
Once you've finished with the sprayed ferns, mount onto cards using spray glue.

## Golden foliage prints

Beautifully elegant and yet super-quick and easy to create, these are ideal for those with long Christmas card lists!

Select your foliage and place under a pile of magazines or books, leaving overnight to flatten.

Spray or hand-paint the foliage with gold paint.

While the paint is wet, carefully press the foliage, paint side down, onto your card.

Pull the foliage directly up to avoid smudging the wet paint.

When dry, finish with self-adhesive gems.

**BUY THE KEY PIECES**
Dark Green cards and envelopes; Black cards and envelopes; Black square cards and envelopes; Gold adhesive gems; spray paint, from a selection, all Hobbycraft

# Card tricks

## HOW TO STITCH CARDS

### Papercut trees

Use off-cuts of patterned card or wallpaper to create stylish cards.

**BUY THE KEY PIECES**
Natural card and envelope; assorted foil print scrap pack; Gutermann metallic thread; cut and emboss flower punch, all Hobbycraft. Papers, The Cambridge Imprint. Small Kraft paper tree; Large Kraft paper tree, both The Danes

**YOU WILL NEED**
- Flower punch
- Assorted scrap paper
- Card and envelopes
- Sewing machine
- Metallic thread

### STEP 1
Use the flower punch to create a row of four circles for the base of your tree.

### STEP 2
Using metallic thread, machine stitch a horizontal line across the centre of the shapes to hold in place.

### STEP 3
Lay further rows that slightly overlap the previous. Create rows in alternating papers that gradually taper in to create a triangular tree shape.

### STEP 4
Once all the rows are stitched in place, finish by stitching a line vertically down the centre of the tree. Pull through the ends to the reverse of the card and trim.

Scandi-luxe cool yule

**WALLPAPER**
Grandeco Tempera wallpaper in Grey, Homebase

**PAINT**
Thrown Clay durable matt emulsion, Ideal Home range at Albany

**FABRIC**
Villandry in Peregrine, Andrew Martin

Christmas doesn't have to be colourful – a pared-back pampas wreath is a great alternative to traditional fir.
**BUY THE KEY PIECES**
Pampas wreath; ribbed table lamp; Black metal vase, all Cox & Cox. Background, Slat Wall in natural oak, NatureWall

# Scandi-luxe cool yule

Embrace a chic twist on classic Scandi seasonal style

**STYLE DIRECTION**

"Hunker down, chalet style, with a bouclé sofa, rich neutrals and touches of jet black and brass for drama"

### Layer it up

Natural textures create an inviting space. Mix plenty of wool, sheepskin and chunky knits for the winter months to stop a neutral scheme feeling too chilly.

**BUY THE KEY PIECES**
Pumpkin sofa, Ligne Roset. Cushion (left), Khalique. Cushion (right), Zoeppritz at Amara. Stanford chair, Jean-Marie Massaud at Poliform. Prop light, Moooi. Print, King & McGaw. Tokki side table, Habitat. Candlesticks, Graham & Green. Mr Zheng coffee table, Lema. Sheepskin rug, Very. New Zealand sheepskin rug, The Conran Shop. Herdwick rug in Grey, Neptune

**BUY THE KEY PIECES**
Wall in (from top) Coco/Graphite; Country Grey; Pure, all chalk paint, Annie Sloan. Try Farringdon luggage rack, Graham and Green. Pine cone, New Covent Garden Market. Wooden star, Very, is similar. Fastnet Stripe stocking, Tori Murphy. Upholstered bench, Ercol. Icelandic sheepskin, The Organic Sheep at Heal's. Notebook, Ban.do. Maronibrater boots, Holland & Holland at Harrods. Calacatta marble flooring, Mandarin Stone.

### Luxe lines
Paint stripes on your walls in varying widths, as well as in three colours (instead of the usual two) for a feature that makes real impact.

**STYLE DIRECTION**
❝ Brown, grey, taupe and charcoal create a warm welcome all year round in the hallway ❞

## Scandi-luxe cool yule

### Side show
Transform a console table with a display of simple paper decs. Hang a wreath from a contrasting frame and a large paper star overhead.

**BUY THE KEY PIECES**
Antique White paper star on wall; White paper star wreath; Black candle holder; brass display box; White paper tree; Rust paper decorations; Antique White paper decorations; Green paper decorations; wooden tree decoration, white wooden tree decoration; ribbed ceramic tree; brass tealight holder; faux fir garland; wooden tray; basket; wooden stool, all Layered Lounge

### CONTRAST VINTAGE WITH MODERN
The simplicity of a neutral scheme sometimes has the potential to feel a little soulless. Counter this by mixing warm blonde woods with darker tones, and show off family heirlooms alongside your favourite high street finds, to create balance and depth.

### INDULGE IN TEXTURE
When it comes to using a sumptuous combination of upholstery fabrics for the Scandi-luxe vibe, linens, velvets and wools are just the start. For extra design points, elevate those textures even more by incorporating embroidery, tufting and tassels on cushions and throws.

### STICK TO SIMPLE SHAPES
Pared-back, contemporary furniture will give any space strong bones and can offer years of versatile service. These simple styles will give you a solid base to work with, then you can ring the changes throughout the different seasons with a few well-chosen accessories.

### ADD GENTLE ACCENTS
With a blend of warm neutrals forming a soothing foundation for your room scheme, opt for nature-inspired accent shades. Try warm pumpkin oranges and olive greens; these will work well with a neutral palette, adding energy but also complementing the laid-back vibe.

# Scandi-luxe cool yule

**BUY THE KEY PIECES**
Black candlesticks; natural wooden bowl; rustic glass vase; White wooden tree decoration; Black round wooden tray; brass candlestick; recycled wood candle holder; slim faux Christmas tree; Black candle holder; brass frill tealight holder; Black display box, all Layered Lounge

## Colour fix
The mix of white, green and copper with wood, wicker and glass makes for the perfect decorative combination this Christmas.

**STYLE DIRECTION**

"Warm up a simple wooden bed with raw linen, then pair with a woven rug and ottoman"

**Paint effect**
Mix two neutrals from the same tonal family to create a textural paint effect.

**BUY THE KEY PIECES**
Salina spindle bed; Salina two-drawer bedside cabinet, both Ercol. For similar bedlinen, try LinenMe

# "I LOVE RUSTIC *Scandi style*"

At Christmas, the neutral monochromes of Tracy Head's modern home are sprinkled with textural seasonal details for a luxe festive look

**ROOM SCREEN**
Creates flexibility in an open-plan space, separating a cosy seating area from the kitchen

## HOME NOTES

### WHO LIVES HERE?
Tracy Head, owner of location house **@ottersbarninteriors**, and her husband Steve, marketing director for a power supply company. They have two sons, Toby and Max.

### THE PROPERTY
Five-bedroomed new-build house in Henley-on-Thames, Oxfordshire.

## "We love spending time together in this room"

'This family seating area adjoins the open-plan kitchen and dining room where, thanks to the sliding door, we each can have our own space but still be together. The exposed beams and trusses here set the style for the house. I balanced the warmth of the wood with a monochrome palette, green-grey slate flooring and weathered metals. The twinkle of candlelight is irresistible at Christmas.'

**BUY THE KEY PIECES**
Bluebell sofa, Sofa.com. Stafford cushion, Sweetpea & Willow, would work here. Try Orion Vision multi-fuel stove, Modern Stoves

'We put our heart and **SOUL** into building a **HOME** that suits the way we want to **LIVE**. 'I love that we are all together at **CHRISTMAS**'

*"I love rustic Scandi style"*

## "The simple flooring style works well"

'Creating schemes for different rooms can throw up a variety of flooring requirements but I wanted a seamless feel throughout. For the linked kitchen, dining and family room, I chose Taj Grey brushed-limestone flooring by Mandarin Stone as it was neither too dark nor too light and had a subtle matt texture, far cosier and more forgiving than a gloss surface. It is also less slippy, making it perfect for our busy family rooms. And, at Christmas time when trees and foliage are brought into the house, falling needles and leaves aren't a problem.'

**BUY THE KEY PIECES**
Taj Grey brushed-limestone floor tiles, Mandarin Stone. The dining table is vintage; try Maddox oak trestle, Dunelm. Try Theodore oak chairs, Perch & Parrow. Fabulous wall light, Rockett St George

## "I blended bespoke with vintage"

'I was very keen to create a unique space for us but it was important that the kitchen was both beautiful and on budget. I went to deVOL for the cabinetry but I was able to source other elements to make it more "me", such as the vintage dining table, which brings that unique one-off feel. The accessories have been collected over the years so the combination of it all feels very considered and carefully put together, rather than all very new.'

**BUY THE KEY PIECES**
The Real Shaker kitchen, deVOL; painted in Hardwick White estate eggshell, Farrow & Ball. Mercury 1200 Induction range cooker, Range Cookers. Try Weathered oak counter stool, Cox & Cox. Stanley medium pendant in polished nickel, Original BTC, has this look. For similar tableware, try The White Company. Sugden & Daughters has a range of vintage and antique kitchenalia

## "Flexibility is important to our family"

'A simple trestle table is perfect for relaxed everyday meal times, and it can also become an impromptu desk for working from home. Covered with a crisp white tablecloth and surrounded by rustic wooden chairs, it is elevated into a fabulous setting for formal Christmas dining.'

**BUY THE KEY PIECES**
For vintage-style road signs, try Craft Heaven Designs on Etsy. For similar crackers, try Fill-Your-Own Fair Isle crackers, Lakeland. Sofia goblet wine glasses, ProCook, are similar

SCANDI CHRISTMAS

> "I use a MIX of my favourite ORNAMENTS and add foliage and nature-inspired ELEMENTS for simple FESTIVE styling"

## "Colours and textures make it cosy"

'With dark paint shades for the walls and a change from limestone tiles to timber flooring, the main sitting room feels incredibly warm and snug, whatever the weather. I brought in a homely touch with a log wall feature and wooden faux shutters.'

**BUY THE KEY PIECES**
Abe chair in Charcoal, Nkuku. Try Staggered log tiles, The Log Basket at Etsy. Try Chantilly seven-drawer chest, Cotswold Company. Try Metal crown, Heavenly Homes and Gardens

## 6 "Two sofas are perfect in this space"

'By choosing a pair of sofas in the same style, plus an armchair, there is lots of room for lounging. This arrangement keeps the seating neat, and it's easy to walk around. I add lots of warm layers with throws and cushions throughout the winter season, and there's always candles on the go for a festive atmosphere.'

**BUY THE KEY PIECES**
Bluebell sofa, Sofa.com. Try Ingrid linen mix in Dove Mist, Ada & Ina, for a similar fabric. Hampton table in Beeswax, Jim Lawrence, would work here. Aegina table lamp, Heavenly Chandeliers, has this look. Try Charcoal linen Terra Fringe cushion cover, LinenMe

## 7 "Add some unexpected elements"

'Creating interesting focal points on the walls was key for this space, to make our new-build home feel more established. Older or reclaimed elements, including pared-back wooden pieces, are important for texture and authenticity, adding comforting elements of nature.'

**BUY THE KEY PIECES**
Metal doors painted in Railings estate eggshell, Farrow & Ball. Try Rustic Grey Stripe grainsack oblong cushion, Maison Brocante

## 8 "I enjoy playing with scale"

'Having a double-height entrance hall means we can have fun with the furnishings. Anything we chose needed to fill the space, otherwise it would have been dwarfed by the ceiling height. I found a cabinet I liked at Kempton Antiques Fair, which the dealer refurbished and painted black. When we brought it home, it was just as I imagined it would be, with loads of storage. Next task was to find the mirror to go above it'

**BUY THE KEY PIECES**
The cabinet is antique; try Antique-style Black multi-drawer storage cabinet, Rocket St George. The Beige arch-shaped mirror, Rose & Grey, would work here. For a similar lamp, try the Cuthbert brass stand, Pooky. Mini faux olive tree, Blooming Artificial, is similar

## 9 "I love making cute seasonal displays"

'I use consoles and trolleys to showcase different finds and artwork, which change with the time of year. I feel it's an organised way to display things rather than dot them around everywhere. In this case, it also gives a wonderful welcome to guests when they arrive in the hallway or on the landing. I've always got next month's flowers and accessories in mind.'

**BUY THE KEY PIECES**
Envostar Stort lamp with wooden frame, Lights.co.uk, has this look. Try Metal storage trolley, The Forest & Co at Notonthehighstreet.com. Cushions in Navy ticking, Ian Mankin

"I love rustic Scandi style"

## "The landing is multi-functional"

'Up here, we wanted to create the same open feel as downstairs, so we have balcony areas and break-out spaces for doing exercise and relaxing. There are nooks with cushions under the dormer windows for curling up with a book.'

**BUY THE KEY PIECES**
Try large Skeleton wall clock in Black/Copper, Barker and Stonehouse. For a similar bag, try Seagrass Grey Star tote, Lescale Furnishings at Etsy. Try Rustic White barn star, Gracie Jaynes

## 11 "We wake up to a lovely view"

'The luxury of designing your own home means you can have a wish list, and a bedroom balcony was on ours. It looks out onto the garden and makes the room feel incredibly spacious. I've kept to a limited pale palette in this room to continue the light, bright feel.'

**BUY THE KEY PIECES**
Hayworth bed in Pewter Grey, Laura Ashley at Next. Try Deuli bed quilt, Nkuku. Try Chantilly Warm White chest of drawers, The Cotswold Company. Walls in Strong White estate emulsion, Farrow & Ball

> "To create a calm, **RESTFUL** home, I have used only three paint shades, while bare **BRICK** and oak, and **VINTAGE** furniture add interest and **TEXTURE**"

*"I love rustic Scandi style"*

**MINIMAL STYLE**
Plain walls help features, such as wooden roof trusses and brickwork, to stand out, while a monochrome palette creates a soothing backdrop for a bathing space

## 12 "We created a bespoke bathroom"

'This space works incredibly hard, as it is also our dressing area with lots of wardrobe storage. Rooflights in the vaulted ceiling means it is flooded with daylight, which elevates the space and gives it a real sense of luxury. I have also added comfortable seating, to create a spa-like space to retreat to.'

**BUY THE KEY PIECES**
La Rochelle cast-iron bateau bath, Cast Iron Bath Company; painted in Downpipe estate eggshell, Farrow & Ball. Try Nero Riven slate flooring, Mandarin Stone. Hampshire mirror in Grey, Brissi. Vintage elm Skinny bench, Design Vintage, has this look

# Scandi-inspired dishes

Whether it's a simple snack or a luxurious cake, why not try these delightful recipes to make your Christmas truly Scandinavian

## 'Easiest-ever Swedish tea ring wreath

Here's how to fake that you can really bake! It's surprising what you can buy in a can these days…

**SERVES 6 | PREP 10 MINS | COOK 15 MINS**

- 50g (1¾oz) pecans, chopped
- 50g (1¾oz) dried apricots, chopped
- 50g (1¾oz) dried mixed fruit
- 50g (1¾oz) dried sour cherries
- 50g (1¾oz) butter
- 50g (1¾oz) light muscovado sugar
- 2tsp cinnamon
- 1 can Jus-rol croissants
- 200g (7oz) fondant icing
- 3tbsp lemon juice
- Edible stars, glacé cherries, to decorate

**1** Heat the oven to 200°C/400°F/Gas Mark 6. Combine the pecans, apricots, dried fruit and sour cherries.
**2** Soften the butter in the microwave for 30 secs, then stir in the muscovado sugar and cinnamon.
**3** Open the can of croissants. Unroll the dough and separate into triangles.
**4** Spread the cinnamon butter mixture over the triangles of dough and scatter over the dried fruit and nut mixture.
**5** From the small side, roll the dough to form crescents. Arrange on a parchment-lined baking tray, with ends touching in a circle. Bake for 15 mins until risen and golden brown. Leave on a wire rack until cool.
**6** Sieve the fondant icing into a bowl, gradually stirring in the lemon juice to make a smooth pouring consistency. Drizzle icing over the wreath, scatter with gold stars and finish with glacé cherries.

## Scandi-inspired dishes

### Berry and walnut toasts

**Using rye bread really amps up the Scandi factor!**

SERVES 6 | PREP 15 MINS | COOK 30 MINS

- 1 medium egg white
- 1tsp coarsely ground cardamom (from 12 pods)
- ½tsp vanilla extract
- 3tbsp golden caster sugar
- Good pinch of sea salt
- 120g (4¼oz) walnut pieces
- 200g (7oz) blueberries
- 6 slices rye bread or sourdough, toasted
- 180g (6¼oz) soft goat's cheese
- Chives, to garnish

**1** Heat the oven to 120°C/250°F/Gas Mark ½. Whisk the egg white, cardamom, vanilla, sugar and salt in a bowl. Stir in the walnuts, then spread them in a single layer on a baking-parchment lined baking sheet. Bake for 30 mins until crisp.
**2** Meanwhile, put the blueberries in a pan with 1tbsp water. Simmer for a few mins until they burst and bleed, stirring occasionally. Sweeten or add lemon juice to taste.
**3** Spread each slice of toast with cheese. Spoon on some blueberries and sauce, scatter with spiced walnuts and sprinkle over sea salt. Garnish with snipped chives.

### COOK'S TIP
If you don't have thickening granules, you can use 2tbsp cornflour mixed with a little water instead.

### 'Lohikeitto' inspired salmon chowder

**Hearty and delicious, this soup is always a warming treat. Look for undyed smoked haddock for the best quality.**

SERVES 4 | PREP 15 MINS | COOK 7 MINS

- 1tbsp olive oil
- 1 onion, peeled and chopped
- 2 sticks celery, chopped
- 1 litre (2 pints) milk
- 4 medium potatoes, peeled and cubed
- 1tbsp thickening granules
- 2x125g (4½oz) smoked haddock fillets, skinned
- 2x 125g (4½oz) salmon fillets, skinned
- 300g (10½oz) frozen sweetcorn
- 2tbsp chopped fresh parsley (optional)

**1** Heat oil in a large pan. Add the onion and celery and cook gently for 10 mins until softened. Pour in the milk, add the cubed potato then bring to the boil. Reduce the heat and simmer for 5 mins. Stir in the thickening granules (or the cornflour mix if you don't have granules).
**2** Add the smoked haddock, salmon and sweetcorn. Simmer for 7 mins until the potatoes are tender. Season to taste. Sprinkle with parsley before serving, if you like.

# Scandi-inspired dishes

## Beetroot knots

The classic and elegant bread rolls you won't be able to resist.

**SERVES 12 | PREP 3 HOURS | COOK 15 MINS**

- 7g (¼oz) sachet yeast
- 300g (10½oz) strong white bread flour
- 100g (3½oz) light spelt flour
- 20g (¾oz) salted butter, softened
- ¼tsp salt
- ½tsp sugar
- ½tsp caraway seeds

**FOR THE BEETROOT PASTE**
- 150g (5¼oz) ready-to-eat beetroot
- 65g (2¼oz) crème fraîche
- 1tbsp horseradish sauce

**FOR THE GLAZE**
- 1 egg yolk, to serve
- Pickled herring
- A few sprigs dill

**1** Mix the yeast with 275ml (9¼fl oz) of tepid water. Add the flours, butter, salt, sugar and caraway seeds into a bowl. Using a mixer with a dough hook, add the water and mix for 10-15 minutes. Pop the dough into an oiled bowl covered with a tea towel, and leave somewhere warm to prove for 1 hour.
**2** To make the beetroot paste, blitz all the ingredients together in a food processor.
**3** Divide the dough in half and tip onto a well-floured surface, knead for a few minutes, then roll each half-batch of dough into a rectangle about 20x25cm (7¾x9¾").
**4** Spread 3tbsp of beetroot paste onto one half, leaving a small border. Place the other half of the dough on top and gently roll out a little. With the dough in landscape, fold the bottom third into the centre, then fold the top third over to meet the other folded end.
**5** Roll out the dough again, now focusing on making it taller. Trim off the rough ends to make the long rectangle neat and cut into 12 strips.
**6** Twist one strip and, holding on to one end, wrap the dough around and tuck the tail under. Repeat with the remaining strips. Put onto a well-floured baking tray. Cover with a damp cloth and leave to prove in a warm place for 1-1½ hours. When you press the dough and it doesn't spring back, it's ready to bake.
**7** Preheat the oven to 240°C/475°F/Gas Mark 9. Bake for 10-12 minutes. Remove from the oven. For the glaze, mix the yolk with 1 tbsp of water and brush over the knots while warm. Serve with the pickled herring and dill.

## Potato and smoked mackerel salad

Give your salad a flavour-packed makeover and boost your omega-3s with this Scandi light bite.

**SERVES 6 | PREP 10 MINS | COOK 20 MINS**

- 1kg (2¼lb) new potatoes, halved
- 170g (6oz) jar cornichons (pickled cucumber), halved
- Bunch spring onions, sliced
- 200g (7oz) radishes, sliced
- 4 smoked mackerel fillets, skinned, broken into pieces
- 2tsp capers
- Small bunch dill, chopped

**FOR THE DRESSING**
- 4tbsp crème fraîche
- 3tbsp mayonnaise
- 2tbsp Dijon mustard

**1** Cook the potatoes in a pan of boiling salted water for 15-20 mins, until tender.
**2** Stir together the dressing ingredients, and season well with salt and pepper.
**3** Drain the potatoes and tip into a bowl. While still warm, add the halved cornichons, sliced spring onions and radishes, and the mackerel, capers and dill. Pour over the dressing and toss together to combine. Serve straight away.

## Spiced molasses layer cake

This layer cake is simple to whip up, but never fails to make a big impact. Decorated with fruit, such as figs and white currants, it has a freshness that is much appreciated at this time of year.

**SERVES 10-12 | PREP 30 MINS | COOK 50 MINS**

- 250g (8¾oz) unsalted butter, plus extra for greasing
- 250g (8¾oz) soft light brown sugar
- 100g (3½oz) blackstrap molasses
- 300g (10½oz) full fat milk
- 350g (10½oz) plain flour
- ¼tsp ground cloves
- ¼tsp ground nutmeg
- 1tsp allspice
- 2tsp bicarbonate of soda
- 2 eggs

### FOR THE ICING
- 180g (6¼oz) unsalted butter
- 375g (13¼oz) icing sugar, sifted
- 180g (6¼oz) cream cheese
- Fresh figs and berries, to decorate

1 Preheat the oven to 180°C/350°F/Gas Mark 4. Grease two 19cm (7½") cake tins and line the bases with baking parchment paper.
2 Melt the butter, brown sugar and molasses in a saucepan over a low heat. Remove from the heat and add the milk, then set aside until lukewarm.
3 Sift the flour, spices and bicarbonate of soda into a large bowl. Make a well in the centre, crack in the eggs and stir to incorporate. Gradually add the melted butter mix, stirring until it forms a smooth batter with no lumps. Divide between the cake tins and bake for 40-50 minutes.
4 Meanwhile, make the icing. Beat the softened butter until very pale, then gradually whisk in the icing sugar until incorporated and smooth. Beat the cream cheese separately, then whisk into the butter icing until very smooth.
5 Once the cakes are cool, cut each in half. Level them off if necessary to ensure they stack securely.
6 To ice, place a cake half on a serving plate or cake stand. Spoon on about 3tbsp of the icing and spread evenly with a palette knife. Repeat with another two halves, then place the final half on top. Spoon a large dollop of icing on the top of the cake and slowly push the icing down the sides with the palette knife, smoothing it as you go with the flat of the knife. Keep adding icing until you achieve the look you are after.
7 To finish, smooth the top of the cake with the palette knife and decorate with the fresh figs and berries.

**COOK'S TIP**
This is best eaten on the day it's cooked, but you can make each element a few days ahead. Assemble when ready to serve.

## Giant cinnamon swirl

Go large with this XL bun, filled with sweetly sliced apples and made using shop-bought brioche dough to speed things up.

**SERVES 12-14 | PREP 1 HOUR 15 MINS | COOK 1 HOUR**

- 4x220g (7¾oz) balls of brioche dough, we used the Northern Dough Co., defrosted if frozen

**FOR THE APPLE FILLING**
- 4 large Braeburn apples, peeled, cored and diced into 6-8mm pieces
- 40g (1½oz) unsalted butter
- 75g (2¾oz) pecans, chopped
- 50g (1¾oz) light brown soft sugar
- 1tsp ground cinnamon
- ¼tsp ground allspice (optional)
- Zest ½ orange
- 50ml (1¾fl oz) brandy or Calvados

**FOR THE CINNAMON BUTTER**
- 75g (2¾oz) unsalted butter, very soft
- 100g (3½oz) light brown soft sugar
- 2tsp ground cinnamon

**FOR THE DRIZZLE**
- 100g (3½oz) icing sugar
- Zest ½ orange
- 2tbsp brandy or Calvados

**YOU WILL NEED**
- 23cm (9") loose-bottomed baking tin, lined with non-stick baking paper

**1** For the filling, put the apples and butter in a large frying pan and cook over a medium heat for 6-8 mins until deep golden and beginning to caramelise. Add the pecans, sugar, spices and orange zest, stir for 1 min until dissolved. Carefully add the brandy and continue cooking for 1-2 mins until syrupy. Set aside to cool.
**2** For the cinnamon spread, in a bowl, cream everything together with a wooden spoon until well combined. Set aside.
**3** Flour a 100cm (3'3") stretch of work surface. Stretch the dough into a long, even piece around 75cm (2'6") long. Use your hands to continue to stretch and flatten it a little so you have a rectangle around 80cm (2'7") long and 15cm (6") wide. Lightly dust with flour, then use a rolling pin to roll it a little thinner, so it's 90cm (2'11") long and 20-23cm (8-9") wide. It's okay if it isn't perfectly rectangle.
**4** Scatter the apples along the length of the dough, around the middle third section. Fold up the bottom third of the dough and press lightly, then fold down the top third to encase. Prick the dough with a fork approximately every 5cm (2"), then press down with your fingers to release any air bubbles.
**5** Spread the cinnamon butter along the entire surface. Loosely roll up the dough from one end to the other to form a large spiral. Transfer to the prepared tin (don't worry if it looks small, it will expand). Cover and leave in a warm place for 30-45 mins, until it has just filled the tin. Heat oven to 200°C/400°F/Gas Mark 6.
**6** Brush the top with milk, avoiding the cinnamon butter. Bake for 20 mins, then cover loosely with a tent of foil before cooking for a further 30-40 mins until cooked through. Press the middle and it should spring back. Remove from the oven and leave to cool for 15 mins.
**7** Whisk together the icing ingredients until smooth. Transfer cake from the tin to a cooling rack, and drizzle over the icing. Leave to cool completely.

# Scandi-inspired dishes

## Herring smørrebrød

A classic Danish open sandwich – perfect for lunch or a light supper.

**SERVES 4 | PREP 20 MINS | COOK 5 MINS**

**FOR THE CUCUMBER PICKLE**
- 4tbsp white wine vinegar
- 1tbsp salt
- 2tbsp caster sugar
- 1tbsp mustard seeds
- 2 star anise
- 1 bay leaf
- 1 cucumber, thinly sliced

**FOR THE BEETROOT DIP**
- 4 cooked beetroot
- 75g (2¾oz) walnuts, toasted
- 1tbsp horseradish sauce
- 1 clove garlic
- 4tbsp crème fraîche

**FOR THE SMØRREBRØD**
- 8 slices rye bread
- 240g (8½oz) jar herrings, drained
- 1 bunch of dill

1 For the pickle, heat all ingredients (except the cucumber) until the sugar has dissolved. Remove from the heat, add the cucumber and leave to one side to cool.
2 To make the dip, blend the ingredients in a food processor until smooth and season.
3 To assemble, spread 2tbsp of the dip on each slice of rye bread and top with the pickle, herring and chopped dill.

## Danish honey cake bars

A delightful sweet treat that goes beautifully with a cup of tea.

**SERVES 12 | PREP 20 MINS | COOK 20 MINS**

- 150g (5¼oz) runny honey
- 45g (1½oz) light muscovado sugar
- 2 medium eggs and 2 egg yolks
- 300g (10½oz) plain flour
- 2tsp bicarbonate of soda
- 1tsp ground ginger
- ¾tsp ground cinnamon
- Pinch of ground nutmeg
- 4 cardamom pods, pods discarded, seeds crushed
- 150g (5¼oz) buttermilk, plus 1tbsp for buttercream

**FOR THE FILLING**
- 150g (5¼oz) butter, softened
- 200g (7oz) golden icing sugar

**FOR THE GLAZE**
- 45g (1½oz) cocoa powder, sieved
- 100g (3½oz) golden icing sugar, sieved
- Gold cake sprinkles (optional)

**YOU WILL NEED**
- 25 x 35.5cm (10 x 14") Swiss roll tin, greased and lined with baking parchment

1 Heat the oven to 160°C/325°F/Gas Mark 3. Put 75ml (2½fl oz) water, honey and sugar in a pan over a low heat to melt, mix well and cool until lukewarm.
2 Using an electric whisk, mix the eggs on a high speed, then gradually add the honey mixture as you keep whisking.
3 Mix the flour with the bicarbonate of soda and spices, sift on to the mixture and then fold in. Add the buttermilk and gently fold in.
4 Scrape into the prepared tin, spreading to the edges and smoothing the top. Bake for 15-20 mins until risen and shrinking away from the edge.
5 For the filling, beat the butter and half the icing sugar with 1tbsp buttermilk until smooth; mix in the rest of the icing sugar until smooth. Leave in the fridge.
6 For the glaze, mix the cocoa and icing sugar in a jug; add 2-3tbsp of hot water to make a sticky glaze.
7 To assemble, cut the sponge in half lengthways, spread the filling over the top of one of the sponges. Top with the other sponge, trim the sides to even, then pour over the glaze and add sprinkles.

**STYLE TIP**
The foliage on this wreath should last a couple of weeks if you keep the Oasis foam in the arrangement well-watered.

# Christmas wreath

Welcome guests with a fresh flower and pine cone arrangement hung on your door

# Christmas wreath

### YOU WILL NEED
- Conifer or spruce cuttings
- Leafy foliage – we used buxus, viburnum and ruscus
- Pine cones
- Spray roses
- Red hypericum
- Holly sprigs with berries
- Florist's scissors
- Buckets
- Cut-flower food (optional)
- Oasis wreath ring (31cm / 12")
- Craft knife
- Green florist's wire
- Wire cutters
- Wide red velvet wired ribbon (optional)

## Conditioning the flowers and foliage

Remove all packaging and ties from the foliage and flowers. Snip away the bottom of the stems by about 5cm (2") and remove any outer petals that look lacklustre from the roses. Fill the buckets with water and a little cut flower food if needed. Strip any leaves from the bottom half of the stems, so no foliage or flowers sit in the water. Place in the water and leave to acclimatise for at least 24 hours. So long as the conifer or spruce is kept cool and dry, you don't need to keep it in the water bucket.

## Preparing the wreath

Fill a large bucket with water and place the Oasis ring on top, allowing it to soak up the water for two minutes. Remove from water and, using a craft knife, cut away the edge of the inner and outer ring. This will help soften the arrangement. If you're planning to hang the wreath, knot the florist's wire in a loop at the top.

**STYLE TIP**
If you can't find the foliage we've used, have a hunt in your garden. Privet hedge cuttings work well as a filler.

## Making the wreath

### STEP 1
Begin with the conifer or spruce cuttings. Snip them down to 15-20cm (6-8") long pieces and remove any needles from the bottom 5cm (2"). Push the cuttings into the foam, all the way around the ring.

### STEP 2
Working with small pieces of leafy foliage, fill any gaps between the conifer or spruce. Vary the size of the leaves to add some interest, making sure to cover the outer sides and the inner ring too. Neaten up any stray pieces by snipping off the excess in order to maintain a circular shape.

### STEP 3
Thread some florist's wire through the base of the pine cones and twist to secure. Position them among the foliage, pushing the wires into the Oasis foam to secure their placement in the wreath. Continue adding pine cones in varying sizes around the wreath.

### STEP 4
Cut the stems of the spray roses to approximately 8cm (3") and push clusters of one, two or three buds into the foam in between the pine cones. Use a mixture of fully bloomed and closed rose heads for variety.

### STEP 5
Add hypericum and sprigs of holly leaves with bright red berries in any noticeable gaps around the wreath, making sure to give the wreath an even mix of green and red colour all over.

### STEP 6
Finally, attach the hanging wire to your front door knocker or finish with a red velvet ribbon tied in a bow to the top for a traditional look.

In order to ensure that your wreath lasts the festive season, be sure to water the foam well, and replace damaged or browning foliage as and when.

75

SCANDI CHRISTMAS

# HOW TO REDUCE Seasonal stress

We speak to the experts for their tips on keeping things simple for a happier festive time this year

**IT'S A WRAP**
Try to do the present wrapping before Christmas Eve so you're not in a huge rush just before the big day

# How to reduce seasonal stress

**T**he rush toward the festive season can feel overwhelming with so much to do, but there are ways to take the stress out of your Christmas prep. We spoke to wellbeing experts to find simple tips to help you plan what you want, get ahead with preparations, and find some much-needed me time amid all the celebrations.

## 1 DO A DECLUTTER

Decluttering may not be the first thing you think of when you're trying to reduce stress, but having some physical, mental and emotional clarity can really help you feel calmer and more in control. 'My advice is to reduce, simplify and plan,' explains psychotherapist, interior designer and declutter expert Helen Sanderson, author of *The Secret Life of Clutter* (published by Little, Brown). 'Remember, the less stuff you have, the less stuff you have to manage, and the simpler your life will be over the Christmas period.'

Helen suggests making time to clear out the clutter that has accumulated over the year. 'A cluttered home is a cluttered mind, but keep your plans simple,' she says. 'Like plants, beautiful things need space to breathe and grow – so do you and so does your home.'

## 2 INVENTORY THE KITCHEN

Once you've cleared unnecessary items out of your home, take a look at what you do need and might be missing. 'Now is a good time to do an inventory of your kitchen to see if there's anything you might require for hosting – a new pan, or some plates, or whatever,' says Beth Kempton, wellbeing author and creator of the award-winning *The Calm Christmas* podcast. 'Make a list ready for the Black Friday and pre-Christmas sales, so you can find a deal.'

## 3 DECIDE ON THE KIND OF CHRISTMAS YOU WANT

There's a lot of pressure to do Christmas a certain way, but letting go of that and instead celebrating in a way that you and your loved ones will truly enjoy, can take a lot of stress out of the festive season. 'Establishing the type of Christmas you want to create and doing it in collaboration with others is key,' explains Helen. 'Sit down with the family, have a conversation and agree who will do what. Explain what support you will need to be able to enjoy the festivities

### HAVE A SOAK
Take time out for yourself so you can relax and unwind, and fully embrace the fun of the festivities light flow through

### WORD GAME
Share your aspirations for the season with family and then write the words onto cards as part of your decorations

> **66** The less **STUFF** you have, the less you have to manage and the **SIMPLER** life is **99**

77
SCANDI CHRISTMAS

## How to reduce seasonal stress

yourself. The conversation will manage the expectations of others. If they're not willing or able to help, explain that you'll need to scale things down so they're manageable.'

**4 WORK OUT YOUR BUDGET**
The cost of living climbs at Christmas, and that financial stress can take the shine off your celebrations. One way to reduce the strain is to plan your spending, so you're less prone to last-minute splurges or panic buying. 'Think about your budget for Christmas. Pick a figure that you would be happy to spend,' says Beth in her podcast. Factor in every extra expense – presents, cards and wrap; going out; festive food and drinks; and travel and accommodation. Once you've added all that up, does the figure match your ideal number? If not, Beth's free downloadable Christmas planner suggests ways to cut down the expense, including reducing the number of people you buy for, spending less on each person or buying joint presents, making your own cards, scaling back on hosting, and even making some gifts and decorations yourself.

'For many of us, giving gifts to those we love is a huge part of the celebration, but it comes from the same pot as everything else we have to fund, so it's worth being aware of what spending the money will stop you doing in other areas.'

**5 PLAN SELF-CARE TIME**
Christmas may be the most wonderful time of the year, but it's also one of the busiest, so make sure you factor in relaxation. 'Make a commitment that you will take a certain number of rest times, and identify exactly what you will do and when they will be,' says Helen. 'That may mean getting up earlier in the quiet hours to take a gentle walk, sitting on your yoga mat before bed, or going to a Pilates class. Set alarms on your phone to remind you to take breaks, and book in a few relaxing activities that will get you out of the house. Only you can prioritise your needs, no one will do it for you.'

**6 LET GO OF PERFECTION**
If your quest for the 'perfect' Christmas means you're too stressed to enjoy it, then take the pressure off. 'The best mantra to combat perfectionism is "Good enough, is enough". Tell friends and family that the priority this Christmas is for quality time, games and conversations, rather than a perfect-looking table and spread,' says Helen. 'Remind yourself that you're an adult now, and that you decide what is good enough.'

**TRY A SPOT OF DIY**
Making your own wreath or table centre adds a personal touch to your home while reducing costs, too

**GIFT GIVING**
Playing Santa can quickly become expensive, so decide on your present-buying budget and try to stick to it

> 66 The priority is QUALITY TIME rather than a perfect Christmas spread 99

78
SCANDI CHRISTMAS

# Budgeting for the festive season

**Ideal Home's columnist and editor of moneyweek.com Kalpana Fitzpatrick shares her financial wisdom**

It's that time of year when households spend hundreds more as they pile up food, gifts and even new things for the home. However, getting a grip on your budget is essential to avoid overspending and a debt hangover in the new year.

Whether you're celebrating Christmas or other festivities, our money expert, Kalpana Fitzpatrick, shares her top tips to help trim costs for the big day.

## MAKE A BUDGET

It's easy to get carried away when shopping for Christmas, so having a strict budget in place is essential to make sure you don't spend more than you should. With just weeks to go, mid-October would be a great time to set a weekly budget – decide on an amount you can afford to spend each week and stick to it.

If you're worried that you may spend more, you could go shopping with a prepaid card such as HyperJar, for example, and only add to it the exact amount you accounted for.

## SAVE FOR THE NEW YEAR

January can be tough for households financially – the wait for pay day is longer (if you got paid early in December) and your finances may be looking a little exhausted after the festivities. To help ease the pressure, if you can, put away a small amount each week into a dedicated savings account until January. Even a small amount like £20 starting in November through to the end of December could leave you with a pot of £160 to kick-start the new year with.

### FIND OUT MORE...

**WORRIED ABOUT DEBT?**
Visit **stepchange.org** for support.

**GET HELP BUDGETING**
Use Money Helper's handy budgeting tool for guidance on how to manage your money: **moneyhelper.org.uk/en/everyday-money/budgeting/budget-planner**

## BLACK FRIDAY

One of the biggest shopping events of the year – Black Friday – takes place on the last Friday in November. It's when most retailers slash prices to encourage people to do their Christmas shopping. Now is a good time to make your wish list and take note of the prices so that you can compare them on Black Friday.

Top tip: I often find Black Friday is the best day to buy at luxury stores that rarely discount their goods, such as Kate Spade for a handbag, Space NK for make-up, or luxury homeware from M&S.

## SIGN UP

This time of the year is a good time to sign up for marketing emails, as many stores will send you their latest deals or discount codes. Some also offer immediate price reductions, such as 10% off your first order, when you sign up – so it's worth doing when shopping online. You can always unsubscribe from any email lists later. You can also earn cashback by shopping via sites like Topcashback or Quidco.

## Do these three things...

### PLAN AHEAD
When you're buying gifts, use Camel Camel Camel (uk.camelcamelcamel.com) to see historical prices on Amazon to check if they're actually a bargain. Use Google Shopping or PriceSpy to compare prices at other stores to find the cheapest deal.

### MAKE A LIST
Know who you are buying for and set a budget against your gift spend. Don't get drawn into spending more than you had planned.

### STOCK UP
If you see non-perishable groceries on offer (look out for things such as cranberry sauce gravy granules or puddings), then buy them now to help keep costs low.

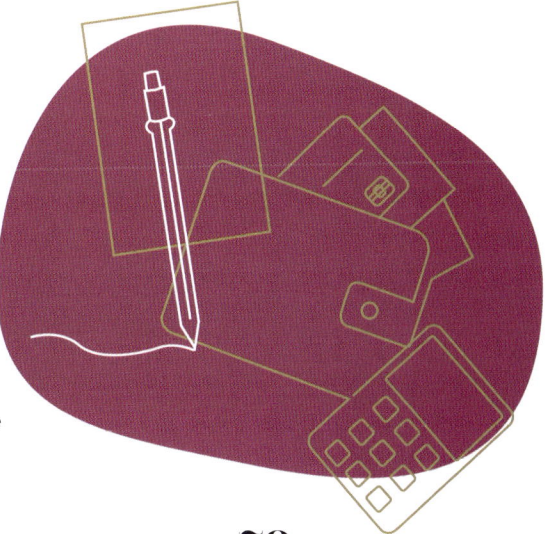

# Line of beauty

Interior designer Justin Coakley transformed a characterless 1930s house, creating a more spacious, welcoming home with a pared-back aesthetic

### Living room

'The build-up to Christmas is the best part – wrapping gifts and putting up decorations; that's the magic of it,' says Justin.

**BUY THE KEY PIECES**
Carlton sofa in White Lazio fabric, BoConcept. Floating Disks side table, West Elm. Christmas tree, The White Company. Bubble chandelier, Dowsing & Reynolds. Shutters, BellaVista Shutters

> "I love **ENGLISH CHRISTMASES**. I was raised in South Africa where it was 35°C, and the last thing you want is a hot dinner. I prefer getting **COSY** and **WARM**, and lighting the fire when it's snowy"

SCANDI CHRISTMAS

'Line of beauty

## HOME NOTES

### WHO LIVES HERE?
Justin Coakley, an interior designer and stylist (**@design_at_nineteen**), lives here with his partner, Zunaid, a doctor, and their whippet, Aalto.

### THE PROPERTY
A 1930s four-bedroom terraced house in south-west London.

## THE LAYOUT

The ground floor has a smart living room with bay window to the front and a large kitchen-diner, with bifold doors which open to the garden at the rear. On the first floor there are two bedrooms, plus a study and bathroom. A second flight of stairs leads to the loft where there is a further bedroom and en suite.

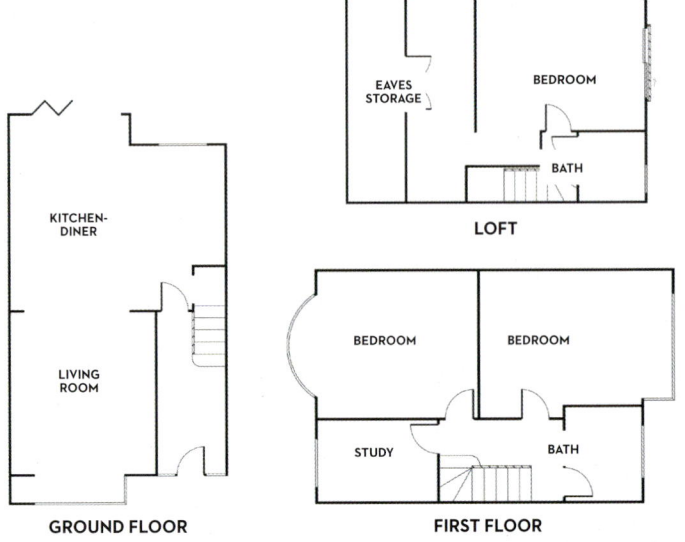

ustin and his partner, Zunaid, wanted a house that they could truly put their stamp on when they first stepped onto the London property ladder. They found it in this neglected 1930s terraced house, taking on an ambitious top-to-bottom makeover to bring back its character, but with a fresh, modern twist.

### WHY DID YOU BUY THIS HOUSE?
'We wanted off-street parking and something that was a project. I'd have loved an Edwardian house, but they were double the price in the area. However, they did try to replicate Edwardian style in 1930s houses. What really sold us was the fact that my partner and I are both over 6ft tall, and the ceilings in this house are 2.8-3m high on the first floor, and the rooms are a really good size.'

### WHAT WORK HAVE YOU DONE?
'It was a complete fixer-upper, so we gutted the house. We lived on the top floor while the basement and ground floor were renovated, and then on the ground floor while the upstairs was renovated. It was manic! What should have been a six-month renovation took a year. We were without a kitchen for months – washing dishes in the bath and microwaving meals. The toilet and bathroom were separate, so we connected them to make a bigger bathroom. We also opened up the living room to make it feel twice the size, and we converted the loft to make a master suite with a separate dressing area. It's gone from two bedrooms and a box room, to a four/five-bedroom house.'

### HOW DID YOU ADD CHARACTER?
'Sadly, the previous owner had ripped out all the period features in an attempt to modernise. That was why I decided to go more contemporary with the interior. The kitchen was very basic, so I redesigned it within an inch of its life and maximised the storage. It's open to the dining area, and when we have guests, I can chat to them across the kitchen island. I use a lot of black accents in my interior designs, which has been a link through all the rooms. I'm all about a minimalist aesthetic that functions; I don't like a lot of clutter everywhere. That is why I have a muted, pared-back scheme using pale, earthy colours, pastelly things and earthy tones.'

### WHY DOES IT WORK FOR YOU?
'Zunaid gives me free rein when it comes to all the interior design. There will be times when he might think something is not a good idea, but he's always amazed when it's done. The renovation is definitely finished – there isn't anything more I can do to it, but it's easy to change the wall colours if I get bored, or move furniture around. For now, we can finally sit and enjoy the space.'

# Line of beauty

**CLEAR VIEW**
Replace a wall between rooms with glazed doors to make it feel open plan and let the light flow through

### 'Living room

'For me, it's about the room functioning well as much as the aesthetic side of it.'

**BUY THE KEY PIECES**
Wicker chair, Cox & Cox; Kubu round chair, Shabby, is similar. Pharaoh rug, West Elm. Wreath, Design at Nineteen and Larry Walshe London. Floor lamp, Tom Dixon

## Kitchen

'The previous owner had knocked the wall down into the kitchen and he had put a very basic kitchen in there. We put in a big central island that is extra deep so it has cupboards front and back.'

**BUY THE KEY PIECES**
Units and work surfaces, Wren; appliances, Neff. Pendant lights, Buster + Punch

## Dining area

'The kitchen is adjacent to the dining area so when we have guests I can chat to them while they're sitting at the table.'

**BUY THE KEY PIECES**
Trestle dining table, John Lewis & Partners. Holland dining chairs, West Elm. For a large dome pendant light, try Etsy

'I planned the layout before we started knocking down walls, making sure furniture would fit'

SCANDI CHRISTMAS

*Line of beauty*

> "As a kid we used to have massive Christmases with 24 people, so it was always mad. Now we keep things **LOW KEY** – our dining **TABLE** only seats six"

**NEAT FINISH**
Shutters complement the streamlined, unfussy décor

## Bedroom

'I am a big fan of Danish and Brutalist design, with quite masculine elements.'

**BUY THE KEY PIECES**
Wardrobe, Lombok; for similar, try the Lynton, Dunelm. Light, Heal's. Walls painted in Duvet Day flat matt, designed by Justin for Coat. Duvet cover set, H&M Home

## Second bedroom

'I like to soften bold lines with organic shapes, muted textures and wood,' says Justin.

**BUY THE KEY PIECES**
Panelling painted in Stone IV, Paint & Paper Library. Rattan bed, John Lewis & Partners. Bedside tables, Home Essentials; for similar, try the Miji, La Redoute. Lounge chair, Srelle. Lamps, Ferm Living at Map Stores. Risbyn paper shade, IKEA

SCANDI CHRISTMAS

*Line of beauty*

'I've maximised the potential for storage in every room. It was all freestanding wardrobes before'

## FOCUS ON...
# CONVERTING A LOFT

*Justin and Zunaid's loft conversion is the perfect relaxing retreat, complete with a well-appointed dressing area. Here's how to achieve it...*

### BOOST LIVING SPACE
A loft conversion is the ideal way to gain extra room without losing any precious garden space. They can often be done under permitted development, so you won't need planning permission.

### LET IN THE DAYLIGHT
The simplest, most affordable loft conversions feature rooflights, bringing in up to three times more natural light than a vertical window of the same size. A dormer-style window will offer more head height.

### MAKE IT MULTI-USE
Plan ahead by creating a space that can be divided into several usable rooms. This master suite with walk-in wardrobe could be adapted to become two bedrooms, appealing to future buyers looking for a family home.

### MAX OUT WALL SPACE
Open shelving can be a better solution than freestanding wardrobes in a loft space, as you can work with the angles and slopes of the ceiling to maximise storage.

### Bathroom
'We had to rip out the new bathroom and have it redone because the builder we hired had done the plumbing incorrectly. The price he quoted was cheaper than anyone else – which proved to be too good to be true.'

**BUY THE KEY PIECES**
Vanity unit, Drench; for similar, try the Crosswater Artist. Mirror, House Doctor at Light & Bay. Floor tiles, Ca'Pietra

'I am **MINIMALIST**. For me, a space has to be **CALMING** and **SERENE**. I love, love, love colour... but in other people's homes

## 'Line of beauty'

**EBONY ACCENTS**
Use black sparingly to ground a neutral scheme – choose thin frames and spindle-leg furniture so as not to overwhelm

### Third bedroom

'Black lines are my signature style as an interior designer; that's the link throughout the rooms,' says Justin. 'I also use a lot of plants, greenery and natural elements.'

Bedside table, West Elm. Wall light, Made. Shelving unit, BoConcept. For a similar wishbone chair, try the Wish, Cult Furniture

## ON SALE NOW!

# Embrace the potential of your humble abode

Struggling for space in your home? You're not alone. In this brand-new title from the makers of Ideal Home magazine, we'll share decorating tips, storage solutions and home hacks to help you make the most of the space you've got!

### Ordering is easy. Go online at:
# WWW.MAGAZINESDIRECT.COM
Or get it from selected supermarkets & newsagents

# Christmas gathering

Collect pine fronds, branches and berries for a rustic Scandi-style Christmas in festive shades of red, white and green

Christmas gathering

Country checks and handpainted plates add freshness to the **TRADITIONAL** red and green festive colour scheme. Add ruby glasses and candles for added twinkle

### FORAGED FEASTING
**BUY THE KEY PIECES**
Foliage, Frida Kim. Swedish clock; dining table; chairs; mirror; chandelier; stemmed glass vases; clear wine glasses; cutwork tablecloth, all from a selection, Maison Artefact. Antique Cranberry wine glasses, from a selection, Lorfords. Scalloped jute rug with Chrysanthemum border, Tate & Darby. Chair seats in Berkeley Sprig in Green, Colefax and Fowler

### GINGHAM & GREEN
**BUY THE KEY PIECES**
Handpainted green plate, The Mews Fabrics & Furnishings. Handmade white porcelain dinner plates; Trefles small saucer by Astier de Villatte, both Summerill & Bishop. Antique monogrammed damask napkins, from a selection, Guinevere Antiques. Gingham crackers, Nancy & Betty. Antique bone inlaid cutlery, stylist's own

91

SCANDI CHRISTMAS

Christmas gathering

'Favour abundance over perfection and capture the **WILD** and tangled **BEAUTY** of fresh-picked pine branches for a wreath or suspended, bauble-strewn branch'

### RAMBLING WREATH
**BUY THE KEY PIECES**
Pine, twig and seed-pod wreath, created by Frida Kim. Red velvet ribbon, from a selection, VV Rouleaux. Antique stone fireplace; pair of antique silvered candlesticks; little felt goat, all from a selection, Maison Artefact. Similar candlestick, from a selection, Baytree Interiors. Clustered paper decorations, from a selection, Toast. 50 warm white LED micro battery outdoor fairy lights, Lights4fun

### COCKTAIL CORNER
**BUY THE KEY PIECES**
Pine branch with antique baubles and velvet ribbon, Frida Kim. Drinks trolley, Vanrenen GW Designs. Crystal ice bucket; silver cocktail shaker, all Guinevere Antiques. (Bottom shelf) Viridian glazed vessel, from a selection, Toad. Presents in wrapped in ivory craft paper, Hobbycraft. Decorated with stamps, from a selection, Blade Rubber Stamps. Ribbon, from a selection, VV Rouleaux. Antique chair; mistletoe print, both Maison Artefact. Striped cushion, Penny Morrison

## Christmas gathering

> "Drape hallways with fir branches to fill your home with Christmas **FRAGRANCE**. Plain and simple paper decorations are all you need to **COMPLETE** the scene"

**STAIRCASE SCENERY**
**BUY THE KEY PIECES**
Pine garland with pine cones, Frida Kim; tied with Callen striped border in Spearmint, Samuel & Sons. Antique silver baubles, from a selection, Maison Artefact. Paper stars, from a selection, Toast. Antique candle sconce, from a selection, Lorfords. Green tapered candles, Curious Egg. Antique foxed mirror; antique painted stool, both from a selection, Maison Artefact. Stool in Cypress linen in Cocoa, Howe at 36 Bourne Street. Wall and woodwork in Stony Ground estate emulsion, Farrow & Ball

**BRANCHING OUT**
**BUY THE KEY PIECES**
Pine branches with red berries, Frida Kim. Mini handpainted red baubles, from a selection; similar basket, large Hogla storage basket, all Toast. Antique silver baubles; stone table; antique urn; antique clock, all from a selection, Maison Artefact. Hampton Scallops Coco scalloped edging, Camilla Hampton Interiors. Walls and shelves in Stony Ground estate emulsion, Farrow & Ball

STYLIST KATRIN CARGILL PHOTOGRAPHS JON DAY FLORAL DESIGNER FRIDA KIM

SCANDI CHRISTMAS

# Handcrafted Christmas

Get creative over the holidays with easy-to-make ideas for lights, decorations and festive trimmings

## Book Christmas tree

**Bring new life to old books by using the pages to create a festive table decoration.**

Take a section of a book and separate off the spine with a craft knife – you will need at least 20 pages.

Taking the first page, fold the leaf in half towards the spine on the diagonal. Stick into place with double-sided sticky tape, then repeat with the other pages.

Once all the pages are folded, gather the edges together and paste with glue. Sprinkle with eco glitter and allow to dry.

Fan out and position on tables when ready.

### YOU WILL NEED
✦ Vintage book   ✦ Craft knife   ✦ Glue
✦ Eco glitter   ✦ Double-sided sticky tape

**BUY THE KEY PIECES**
Card, glitter and glue, Hobbycraft. Paper and trims, from a selection by The Danes and Cambridge Imprint. Glasses, from a selection by Emma Britton. Plates, from a selection at Sainsbury's

# Handcrafted Christmas

**BUY THE KEY PIECES**
Wreath, wooden beads, wire, paint, glitter and glue, all Hobbycraft. Ribbon, from a selection at Jane Means

## Pine cone wreath

**Make a wonderful decoration with gathered pine cones.**

Paint your wreath and cones with white paint. When dry, dab the ends of the pine cones with glue and sprinkle with eco glitter.

Glue the cones on to the wreath. When firmly fixed, thread wooden beads on to acrylic wire and tie to the wreath between the cones.

Push eucalyptus leaves around the wreath, and finish with a ribbon.

### YOU WILL NEED
✦ Grapevine wreath ✦ Pine cones ✦ White paint
✦ Liquid glue ✦ Eco glitter ✦ Glue gun
✦ Wooden beads ✦ Acrylic wire
✦ Real or faux eucalyptus ✦ Ribbon

# Handcrafted Christmas

**BUY THE KEY PIECES**
Wood dowel and twine, both Hobbycraft. Beads, Jane Means.

**STYLE TIP**
The stars look lovely hung in a window for passers-by to enjoy. Or suspend them in a stairway and follow the stars at bedtime.

## Natural stars

Hang a star to lead the way to Christmas.

Arrange the dowels into a star shape and wrap the ends together with florist's wire.

Add beads or faux berries to one side with more wire.

Finish with a sprig of eucalyptus to dress the star.

### YOU WILL NEED
✦ Wooden dowels, cut to size
✦ Florist's wire or twine ✦ Beads
✦ Thread ✦ Real or faux eucalyptus

## Dressed up dome

A wonderful way to present gifts for guests in a hallway.

Wrap parcels in co-ordinating paper and ribbon. Keep a tonal colour code in mind to make the gifts look good together and use double-sided tape for neatness.

Stack up inside the dome and add a mini tree for that almost-under-the-tree moment.

Cover with the dome, using cloths or gloves to prevent finger marks and smudges.

### YOU WILL NEED
✦ Gifts ✦ Wrap ✦ Ribbon ✦ Double-sided tape
✦ Glass dome ✦ Bristle tree decoration

**BUY THE KEY PIECES**
Glass dome, Lights4fun. Bristle tree, Hobbycraft. Paper and trims, from a selection by The Danes and Cambridge Imprint

## Paper stocking

Why struggle with wrapping awkward presents when you can put them in a paper stocking?

Draw a stocking-shaped template on to card and cut out.

Place it on to your chosen paper and draw around – you'll need to put the template on the right side of one piece of paper and the wrong side of the other, so the stocking shape matches up.

Cut out. Join the 'seams' either with double-sided tape or by using a hole punch along the edge and then threading through with ribbon.

Add crafted paper ruffles, pom-poms and ribbon trim, then fill with presents.

### YOU WILL NEED
✦ Card for a template ✦ Paper – gift wrap or wallpaper offcuts are ideal ✦ Double-sided fixing tape ✦ Eco glitter ✦ Ribbon and trim

**BUY THE KEY PIECES**
Paper and trims, from a selection by The Danes, Jane Means, Cambridge Imprint and Hobbycraft

*Handcrafted Christmas*

### ✧ Frosty lanterns

Invest in solar-powered lights and use the winter sun to create the loveliest lighting.

Cut your glitter tape into narrow triangles and stick on to the lanterns to create sparkly icicles.

Place a bristle tree inside and watch it light up in the dark.

#### YOU WILL NEED
✦ Solar-powered jar lights ✦ Glitter tape ✦ Miniature Christmas trees

#### STYLE TIP
As these are solar powered, they're perfect for an open porch as they will start to glow as night falls. Or carry them as you go carol singing!

**BUY THE KEY PIECES**
Glitter tape and bristle trees, Hobbycraft. Trims, from a selection by The Danes, Jane Means and Cambridge Imprint

FEATURE AND STYLING SARA BIRD PHOTOGRAPHS DAN DUCHARS

# White Christmas

Emma and Ant's elegant home may be all serene shades of cream and white, but that doesn't mean it's not made for festive family fun

# 'White Christmas

### 'Living room
'The travertine table was a worthwhile investment – I fall in love with it again every day when I sit here in the mornings.'

**BUY THE KEY PIECES**
Try the Beige octagonal table, Pamono. Wishbone chairs, Aram. Baubles, from a selection, Heavenly Homes & Gardens. Sofa (left), reupholstered by Edwards Upholstery in a Bute Fabrics material

**WINDOW UPDATES**
Old metal frames were swapped for more traditional wooden sashes and decorative cornicing was reinstated

# 'White Christmas

## HOME NOTES

### WHO LIVES HERE?
Emma Grant, founder of a sheepskin baby brand, her husband Ant Long, a lawyer, and their three children.

### THE PROPERTY
A double-fronted Victorian villa in east London.

Emma and Ant found out they were expecting Otto, their first son, the day they exchanged on the house and nearly pulled out. The house had a 1970s vibe – but not in a good way – when they bought it, so they embarked on a top-to-toe refurbishment, replacing windows, flooring and period features, as well as adding a kitchen extension and reconfiguring the upstairs to create a family bathroom and en suite.

### WHERE WERE YOU LIVING BEFORE?
'We were previously living more centrally in the city, but by moving out a bit, we've gained masses of extra space and the benefit of a large country-style garden full of pear trees. I'm so glad we didn't pull out of the sale – despite the chaos of a renovation with a newborn.'

### HOW DID YOU MANAGE THE WORK?
'We had hoped the house would be habitable before Otto's birth, but he was five months old when we finally moved back in, albeit without a kitchen or half the extension yet built. We had a makeshift kitchen in what is now the playroom and I used the garage as a design studio/warehouse for my brand Binibamba (binibamba.com), which I had set up at the same time.'

### WHAT IS YOUR DECORATING STYLE?
'I'm a sucker for a neutral… probably beige and white together. It may sound boring, but I *love it*. When creating the decorating scheme, there were lots of moodboards and magazine tear sheets, and I did a lot of Instagram browsing. The rabbit hole was deep, plus there were endless trips around showrooms.'

### WHAT HAVE YOU LEARNT?
'Plan and design for the life you lead and the home you want to build. There's no point having a show home or being too precious, but there's still room to have some lovely pieces even with kids roaming free.'

### WHAT WOULD YOUR DREAM HOME BE LIKE?
'We love this house so much. If we could put it on roller skates to the countryside one day and do the loft, we could live here forever. We have so much talent nearby and used lots of local craftspeople including a joiner, upholsterer and the sign writer who made our door number. These people made the house so special.'

### WHAT DOES CHRISTMAS MEAN TO YOU?
'Excitement levels sky high, sugar rushes, and little people pulling baubles from the tree. The house comes alive! We love entertaining and had our entire families for Christmas in our first year here. There were 18 round the dining table. It was totally mad, but totally magic.'

# 'White Christmas

### 'Living room

'All the original fireplaces had been stripped out, but we found some great local period pieces to use as substitutes.'

**BUY THE KEY PIECES**
Tree, from a selection, The White Company. Tree decorations and lights, from a selection at Cox & Cox, and Heavenly Homes & Gardens. Wreath, Sage Flowers.

**WALL HANGING**
The front door isn't the only place for a wreath – here it adds some unexpected detail to the fireplace

*White Christmas*

### Dining area

'We put in a big picture window to connect to the outside. This space is the hub of our home, and there is a long window seat – it's amazing how many people we can squeeze in for dinner!'

**BUY THE KEY PIECES**
Vintage floor lamp, from a selection, McCully & Crane. Mila wine glasses, Nkuku. Flowers, Sage Flowers

> "We used CREATIVE thinking to get things DONE within our budget"

## Kitchen

To get the look for less, Emma and Ant had the island wrapped in MDF-skimmed concrete rather than choosing a solid slab.

**BUY THE KEY PIECES**
Kitchen in Cabbage Patch Green, British Standard. Worktops (on main units) and splashback, J&R Marble. Whitewashed oak floor, Angelo Flooring

**LOW LIGHT**
Make a feature of a pendant by hanging it on a long cable above an island

### Child's bedroom

'This room was designed as a relaxing respite from the busyness of the playroom. The theory is, it encourages sleep!'

**BUY THE KEY PIECES**
Walls in Wimborne White modern emulsion, Farrow & Ball. For a similar look, try Ocana checked rug, La Redoute. Mamabear sheepskin teddy (on bed), Binibamba

> " Our home is our happy SANCTUARY away from the WORLD "

'White Christmas

## FOCUS ON... TRAVERTINE

*Emma's stylish home has several pieces made from this natural stone. Here's what you need to know...*

✦ Travertine is a natural material that can be used to make furniture, tiles, flooring or splashbacks. Each piece is unique and it can sometimes have a very rustic appearance, although it's possible to find polished pieces for a more modern look. It's a cheaper alternative to marble.

✦ Travertine makes a good choice for bathrooms, as it's non-slip, water-resistant and can be used in the shower or around taps when sealed. This also makes it ideal as a kitchen splashback or flooring in a hallway.

✦ Like many natural stones, travertine requires regular cleaning with gentle dish soap. Harsh chemicals or anything abrasive must be avoided. Travertine needs to be sealed when installed and resealed periodically to protect it, as it can be easily damaged with scratches.

✦ For a more family-friendly option, try travertine-effect tiles or concrete furniture, which has a similar look.

### 'Nursery

'Rather than go for a colourful scheme, I think that a neutral room is more calming for babies – so long as there is lots of interest and detailing for them to focus on.'

**BUY THE KEY PIECES**
Walls painted in Shadow White modern emulsion, Farrow & Ball. Ila y Ela raffia hanging lion (on wall), Smallable. Sheepskin items, all Binibamba

### Study area

'Originally, this space was planned as the dining area, but now it provides a little oasis of calm before you reach the kitchen, where all of our family life unfurls.'

**BUY THE KEY PIECES**
La Redoute's Jimi vintage-style desk, is a similar shape. For a similar vintage lamp, try Pamono. The Tipped Icelandic sheepskin rug, Idyll Home, has this look

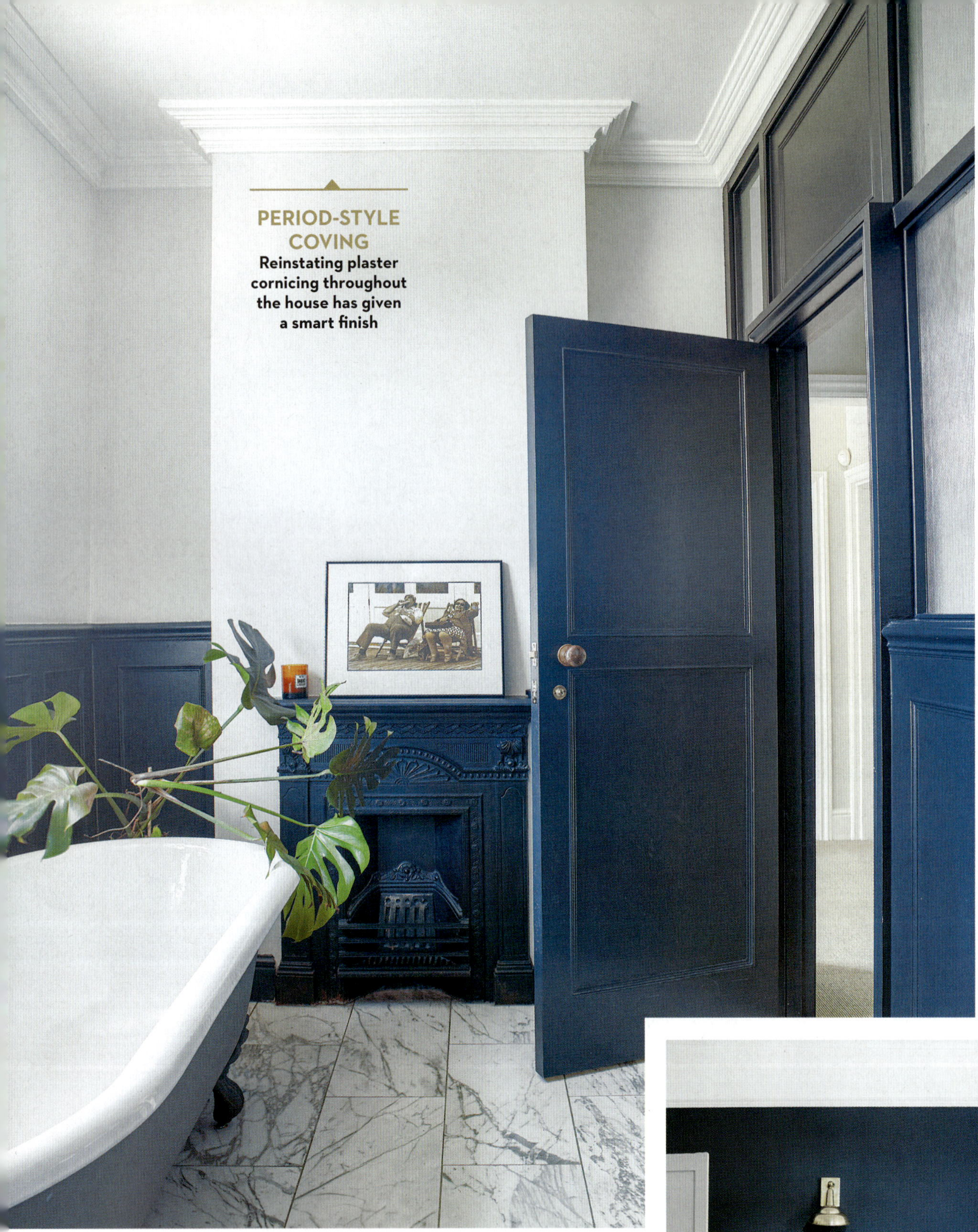

**PERIOD-STYLE COVING**
**Reinstating plaster cornicing throughout the house has given a smart finish**

## 'Family bathroom

'We swapped a bedroom for this space and added reeded glass to allow in light from the landing.

**BUY THE KEY PIECES**
Roll-top bath, from a selection, Aston Matthews. For similar marble-effect floor tiles, try Volterra Tortona Matt, Fired Earth

## 'Main bedroom

'Using a dark shade and keeping the space unadorned makes our room feel calm and grounding.'

**BUY THE KEY PIECES**
Wall in Railings modern emulsion, Farrow & Ball. For a similar wall light, try Whizzer, Pooky. The Ascot bed in Natural, Dusk, has a similar look

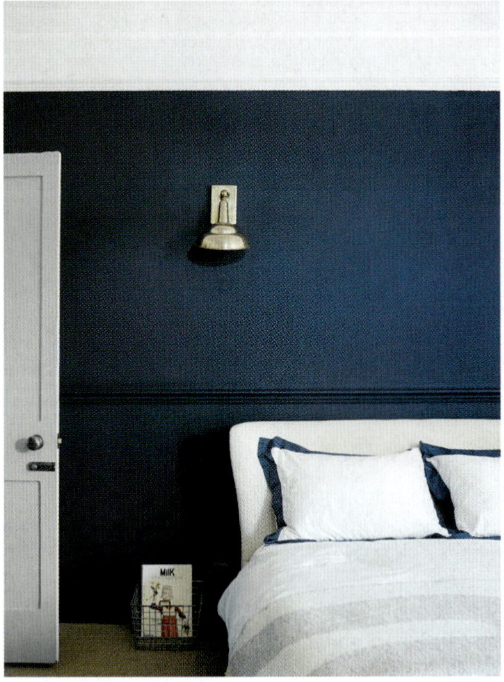

**FEATURE** MARY WEAVER **PHOTOGRAPHS** MARY WADSWORTH **STYLING** REBECCA DE BOEHMLER
**STYLING ASSISTANTS** AVA DE LA FLOR AND ISABELLA CHARLESWORTH **FLOWERS** SAGE FLOWERS

## ON SALE NOW!

# Embrace simplicity and serenity in your home

Home trends come and go, but the Scandi vibe is here to stay. Explore some of our favourite Scandinavian-inspired homes, and discover how to update the traditional Scandi aesthetic for a more contemporary feel.

### Ordering is easy. Go online at:

# WWW.MAGAZINESDIRECT.COM

Or get it from selected supermarkets & newsagents

# The personal touch

Get crafty with edible decorations this Christmas – perfect for decorating the house or gifting to friends and family

# The personal touch

## Best ever gingerbread dough

This recipe is the only one you'll need for all your gingerbread craft needs. It bakes crisp and strong, making it perfect for everything from decorations to gingerbread houses.

**MAKES 16-20 BISCUITS | PREP 10 MINS | COOK 10-12 MINS**

- 100g (3½oz) salted butter
- 1tbsp golden syrup
- 50g (1¾oz) dark muscovado sugar
- 50g (1¾oz) light muscovado sugar
- ¼tsp bicarbonate of soda
- 1tbsp ground ginger
- 1tsp ground mixed spice
- 225g (8oz) plain flour

**YOU WILL NEED**
- Festive cookie cutters (optional)

**1** Melt the butter, golden syrup and both dark and light muscovado sugars in a pan over a medium heat, stirring until smooth. Sift in the remaining ingredients, then mix well to form a soft dough.
**2** Flatten the dough into a disk and wrap well in cling film. Chill for at least 1 hour or up to 2 days. Alternatively, freeze for up to 3 months to use at a later date.

### VARIATIONS
**MAKE IT VEGAN**
Swap butter for a plant-based alternative, such as Stork or Naturli baking block.
**MAKE IT GLUTEN-FREE**
Swap the plain flour for a gluten-free plain flour blend.

**COOK'S TIP**
If shaping/baking straight away, roll the dough between two sheets of baking paper while still warm. Slide onto a tray and chill until firm. It will cool faster and require less elbow grease to roll.

## Royal icing

The trick to perfectly iced cookies is getting the icing consistency right. This recipe is very forgiving, so play around with the consistency, simply add a little more water if it's too stiff, or more icing sugar if too runny.

**MAKES ABOUT 300g | PREP 10 MINS**

- 250g (8¾oz) pure icing sugar, sifted
- 1 medium egg white
- ½tsp lemon juice

**YOU WILL NEED**
- Electric hand whisk or food processor

**1** Sift the icing sugar into a mixing bowl. Add the egg white and lemon juice, then whisk with an electric hand whisk on a low speed for 2-3 mins until it becomes smooth. It should be thick but spreadable. If it looks dry and crumbly, whisk in a few more drops of water. If it looks runny and glossy, mix in a little extra of the icing sugar.
**2** Transfer to a bowl and cover with a damp cloth to prevent it from drying out. The icing will keep for up to 1 week, stored in an airtight container in the fridge. Use the icing as it is to stick gingerbread pieces together or thin with a little water for decorating biscuits (see below) and cakes.

### VARIATIONS
**MAKE IT VEGAN**
Swap egg white for 2-3tbsp aquafaba (the liquid from a can of chickpeas).

### CONSISTENCY ADVICE
**FOR PIPING (border, writing and fine decoration)**
Add a little water to the icing, a few drops at a time until it's thick but flows easily. It should be drizzleable but hold its shape and not spread or run when piped.
**FOR FLOODING (filling the biscuits for a fully iced finish)**
Add more water to the icing to reach a pourable consistency. To test its consistency, use a spoon to drizzle the icing back into the bowl. It should settle back into a smooth surface within several seconds but still have some body.

SCANDI CHRISTMAS

## The personal touch

**COOK'S TIP**
If you're not keen on piping your festive greetings, let the cookies dry completely, then use an edible pen to write your messages.

### Tasty gift tags

These sweet little decorations will add a real personal touch to your gift wrapping.

**MAKES 20-30 | PREP 45 MINS | COOK 10-12 MINS**

- 1 portion gingerbread dough
- 1 potion royal icing
- Gel food colouring

**YOU WILL NEED**
- Festive cookie cutters
- Piping bags

**1** Heat the oven to 190°C/375°F/Gas Mark 5. Roll the gingerbread dough on a lightly floured surface to about 5mm (¼") thickness. Use a sharp knife to cut the dough into small rectangles about 10x5cm (4x2"), then cut the corners off one end to fashion into a gift tag shape. Alternatively, cut out any shape you prefer using festive cookie cutters.
**2** Use a 1cm (½") piping nozzle or straw to punch out a hole in each cookie for threading later, then arrange, well spaced on lined baking trays. Bake for 10-12 mins until firm and slightly darkened (they will harden as they cool). Leave to cool on trays.
**3** Divide the icing between two bowls. Adjust the consistency of one portion for piping and the other for flooding (see p113 for recipe). Colour about one-third of the piping icing (we went with a classic Christmas red), then transfer all three portions to separate piping bags.
**4** Snip the ends off the piping bags to make a very small hole and use the thicker white icing to pipe a border around the cookies and around the hole too. Set aside for 5 mins to harden a little, then use the thinner flooding icing to fill. Use a toothpick to spread the icing to create a smooth, thin and even layer. Set aside to dry for at least 1 hour.
**5** Use the coloured icing to carefully write festive greetings onto the tags. Set aside to dry completely – at least 4 hours or ideally overnight. Thread with ribbon or string and use to decorate your presents.

**COOK'S TIP**
Keep an eye on the cookies in oven as sweets can bubble and discolour quickly.

### Stained glass decorations

Get the whole family involved in these delicious alternatives to traditional tree decorations.

**MAKES ABOUT 16 DECORATIONS | PREP 30 MINS PLUS COOLING AND DRYING | COOK 12-14 MINS**

- 1 portion gingerbread dough
- 8-10 colourful hard sweets (we used jolly ranchers), finely crushed
- 1 potions royal icing
- Gel food colouring

**YOU WILL NEED**
- Festive cookie cutters
- Piping bags
- Ribbon or string

**1** Heat the oven to 190°C/375°F/Gas Mark 5. Roll the gingerbread dough on a lightly floured surface to about 5mm (¼") thickness. Cut out festive shapes of your choice. Use small cutters to make a hole or two in the cookies, then use a 1cm (½") piping nozzle or straw to punch a hole in the top of each for stringing.
**2** Arrange the cookies on lined trays and bake for 8 mins. Remove from the oven and carefully spoon a small mound of the crushed sweets into the holes. Return to the oven for 3-4 mins until the sweets have melted and spread to fill the hole. Leave to cool completely.
**3** Adjust the consistency of the icing for piping (see p113 for recipe), then colour as liked. Transfer the icing to piping bags and decorate the cooled cookies as desired. Set aside to dry for at least 4 hours or overnight, then thread with string or ribbon for hanging.

114

SCANDI CHRISTMAS

**COOK'S TIP**
For a firmer hold for hanging, use edible glue when making the wreath.

## Edible wreath

A gingerbread wreath makes a beautiful addition to your festive decorations and a thoughtful gift that won't break the bank.

**MAKES 1 SMALL WREATH | PREP 45 MINS PLUS COOLING AND DRYING | COOK 25 MINS**

- 2 portions gingerbread dough
- 2 potions royal icing
- Gel food colouring

**YOU WILL NEED**
- Festive cookie cutters
- Piping bags

**1** Heat the oven to 190°C/ 375°F/Gas Mark 5. Roll the gingerbread dough on a lightly floured surface to about 5mm (¼") thickness. Using cookie cutters, cut out festive shapes of your choice.

**2** Arrange the cookies on lined trays and bake for 10-12 mins. Gather and re-roll the offcuts to about 1cm (½") thick and at least 25cm (10") diameter. Cut a large disc, about 25cm (10") across, using a bowl as a guide. Cut a hole in the centre about 15cm (6") across, creating a doughnut. Transfer to a baking tray and bake for 15-18 mins until firm. This will form the base for the wreath.

**3** Set one-third of the icing aside and adjust the consistency of the rest for piping (see p113 for recipe). Divide between small bowls and colour as liked. Transfer to piping bags and pipe the gingerbread cookies with decorative icing. We went with simple line and dot patterns for a modern look, but do as you like. Set aside to dry for at least 4 hours or ideally overnight.

**4** Use the reserved icing to 'glue' the gingerbread to the large disk, layering as you go. Set aside to dry for at least 4 hours, then string with ribbon for hanging.

# 'It's a wrap

Be inspired and get creative with our six stylish 'no waste' Christmas wrapping ideas. From brown paper packages to gifts tied in fabric off-cuts, the results are beautiful and sustainable

### Draw on brown paper

Create a super-cute 'driving home for Christmas' wrap. Start by wrapping your gift in brown paper and then simply draw your own unique vehicle design directly onto the paper, using marker or metallic pens. Pop a small wire Christmas tree on the top and tie with cotton stripy string. stick-on gems. Christmas Kraft tape adds the final festive touch.

**STYLE TIP**
Sketch out your drawing in pencil, then go over it in black marker once happy with the design.

**BUY THE KEY PIECES**
Kraft paper roll; Woodland Scenics soft flake artificial snow, both Hobbycraft. Conifer model tree packs, 4D Modelshop. Cotton stripy string in Red/White, RE. Compact naked wire lights, Cox & Cox

'It's a wrap

### Utilise fabric off-cuts
Put fabric remnants to good use and create linen cloth-tied presents. Adorn with clear baubles filled with winter foliage for a fresh take on seasonal wrapping.

**BUY THE KEY PIECES**
Fabrics from top left: Air Natural wide-width linen sheer; Offline Vellum wide-width linen sheer, both Mark Alexander. Pure Willow Boughs Embroidery in Paper White, Morris & Co. Fillable baubles, Hobbycraft. Compact naked wire lights, Cox & Cox. Rectangular jute rug in Stone Grey, Rowen & Wren

*'It's a wrap*

**STYLE TIP**
Use silk, velvet or chiffon ribbon to add a touch of glamour to this simple wrap.

**Add old book script to your wrap**
Pages from old books make beautiful wrapping papers. Combine script of a different scale for gift tags as an added decorative touch.

**BUY THE KEY PIECES**
Old books, from charity shops. Flax string, RE. Squish-a-Lazy footstool in Cucumber Sandwich clever velvet, Loaf

### Recycle paper gift bags

Add glitz to gifts using gold and white striped paper bags. Punch a row of holes along the top edge to thread through gold raffia or velvet ribbon in a contrasting colour for a simple finishing touch.

**BUY THE KEY PIECES**
Gold and White striped treat bags, Hobbycraft. Plum velvet ribbon, VV Rouleaux. Gold raffia paper ribbon, Nancy & Betty. Circular labels made from A6 flat cards, Paperchase. Gold eucalyptus garland; Skylar set of two coffee tables (smaller shown), both Graham & Green

### 'Use up leftover lining paper

Lining paper acts as the perfect foil to a shimmering sprayed fern frond. Simply spray-paint a clean, dry leaf and secure in place with a gold buckle and length of velvet ribbon for an elegant seasonal flourish.

**BUY THE KEY PIECES**
Smooth-grade lining paper, B&Q. Fern frond painted in Artisan Copper Effect paint, Craig & Rose. For similar buckle, try Liberty. Velvet ribbon, John Lewis & Partners. Hay Phi scissors, Trouva. Squish-a-Lazy footstool in Cucumber Sandwich clever velvet, Loaf

## HOW TO CRAFT BOX

### Give papier mâché boxes a twist

Embellish papier mâché boxes with lengths of hessian and add sprigs or mini wreaths of rosemary for a festive look that is natural and easy to achieve.

**BUY THE KEY PIECES**
Square Kraft papier mâché box; papier mâché heart boxes; hessian roll, all Hobbycraft. Circular labels made from A6 craft card, The Paperbox. Hay utility scissors, eBay. Skylar set of two coffee tables (smaller shown), Graham & Green

### YOU WILL NEED
- Roll of hessian
- Kraft papier mâché box(es)
- Scissors
- Double-sided tape
- Card
- Metallic pen or marker
- Sprigs of rosemary
- Florist's wire

## 'It's a wrap

### STEP 1
Cut two lengths of hessian, long enough for each to wrap around the sides of the box. Secure both ends to the top with double-sided tape.

### STEP 2
Cut a circle from the card to make the label. Place in the centre on top of the attached hessian. Use your pen of choice to write on the label.

### STEP 3
Gently bend the rosemary sprig to form a mini wreath shape and secure the ends with florist's wire. You may need to join two sprigs together. Tape in place.

# THE A-Z OF Scandi brands

From iconic chairs to sleek storage and elegant kitchenware, these brands champion Scandinavian design

### for AUDO COPENHAGEN

If you're a fan of refined Nordic interiors, Audo Copenhagen should definitely be on your radar. This Danish family business is rooted in the principles of Scandinavian design: simplicity, quality, and purpose. Expect sleek silhouettes, tactile materials and an enduring, minimalist aesthetic from a product portfolio that includes furniture, lighting and accessories. Collaborations with creative names like Colin King and Norm Architects mean collections are seriously covetable, from sculptural candle holders to architectural sofas. At the heart of the brand is Audo House, a beautifully curated hybrid space in Copenhagen that blends showroom, concept store, café, hotel and event facilities – offering a living, breathing expression of the brand's ethos.

**Designed for Audo Copenhagen by Ib Kofod-Larsen, the Knitting Chair is available at nest.co.uk**

### for BLOOMINGVILLE

Founded in 2000 by Danish designer Betina Stampe, Bloomingville has grown from a small start-up into a major player on the global interiors scene – all while hanging onto its joyful, lived-in spirit. Bloomingville's signature look blends earthy tones, tactile textures and a touch of rustic charm, making it easy to add warmth and personality to your space. From lamps to decorative sculptures, woven baskets and patterned stoneware, their ever-evolving collection feels fresh, accessible and full of cheer. Whether you're styling a shelf, hosting friends, or refreshing a child's bedroom, there's a playful practicality at the heart of everything Bloomingville creates. Designed to be mixed, matched and made your own, these are mood-lifting pieces that celebrate everyday living. You'll find Bloomingville stockists throughout the UK and online.

A modern classic, the award-winning Block Lamp, designed by Harri Koskinen Design House Stockholm

## for CARL HANSEN & SØN

Few names are as synonymous with Danish craftsmanship as Carl Hansen & Søn. A family-run design house with over a century of history, the brand has mastered the art of creating furniture that's both timeless and heavily committed to sustainability. Now led by third-generation owner Knud Erik Hansen, the company works with influential contemporary designers while continuing to manufacture pieces designed by some of the most iconic Scandinavian names, including Hans J. Wegner, Arne Jacobsen, Børge Mogensen and Kaare Klint. But this isn't just about pretty silhouettes. The brand's ethos is all about longevity, both when it comes to style and sustainability. Protecting the planet is integral to its approach: materials are responsibly sourced, craftsmanship is prioritised over mass production, and each design is made to stand the test of time. Carl Hansen & Søn's furniture is sold worldwide, and you'll find the UK's flagship store in London's Belgravia.

## for DESIGN HOUSE STOCKHOLM

Design House Stockholm isn't your average design brand – it's more like a curated gallery of ideas. Rather than setting a house style, they collaborate with up-and-coming and established designers to bring their innovative concepts to life. The result? A covetable collection of Scandinavian design pieces, spanning everything from lighting to plant pots, rugs and tableware. It was Design House Stockholm which championed Harri Koskinen's cult Block Lamp series (a light bulb frozen in a glass "ice cube") and the now-legendary Knot cushion by Icelandic designer Ragnheiður Ösp Sigurðardóttir. Playful, bold and instantly recognisable, these pieces are as much talking points as they are functional homeware. Design House Stockholm has also collaborated with well-known designers, including Alexander Lervik, Lena Bergström and Catharina Kippel. The term 'Scandinavian' refers to the brand's philosophy and aesthetic perspective, rather than geography and nationality, with French, German, Australian, American and Chilean designers in their network.

Colourful tableware and vases from Bloomingville

## for EIKUND

If you love clean lines and timeless design, make sure Eikund is on your radar. This Norwegian brand was launched in 2016 with a clear mission: to breathe new life into pieces by Norwegian design icons, such as Fredrik A. Kayser and Torbjørn Bekken (whose striking 1960 Veng bar stool has recently been reissued). But Eikund is about more than just beautiful furniture. Sustainability is woven into every step of their process, from responsibly sourcing raw materials to reducing $CO_2$ emissions and limiting the use of toxic chemicals. Their commitment to quality means every piece is built to last, an antidote to fast furniture trends. Even behind the scenes, Eikund champions ethical partnerships and a people-first approach. The result is Nordic modernism at its best: simple, enduring, and consciously made. With their thoughtful reimagining of vintage silhouettes, Eikund not only honours Norway's design heritage but brings it firmly into a more sustainable future.

## The A–Z of Scandi brands

### F for FRITZ HANSEN

Few design brands can lay claim to shaping modern interiors quite like Fritz Hansen. Founded in Copenhagen in 1872, the Danish powerhouse has spent over 150 years collaborating with design legends – from Arne Jacobsen to Poul Kjærholm – to produce some of the most recognisable furniture of the 20th century, including the swan-like curves of the Egg Chair and the endlessly versatile Series 7™ Chair. But Fritz Hansen isn't stuck in the past. Recent collaborations with contemporary designers keep the brand looking forward, with elegant new takes on classic silhouettes and beautifully crafted collections encompassing everything from cushions to outdoor furniture, storage, lighting and kitchen accessories. The latest collection, Skagerak, features contemporary wooden furniture co-created with renowned architects and designers.

▸ Fritz Hansen's Series 7™ Dining Chair in Coloured Ash by Arne Jacobsen. Available at nest.co.uk

### G for GEORG JENSEN

Best known for its sleek silverware, Georg Jensen's story began back in 1904 when the nature-loving silversmith lived just north of Copenhagen. Surrounded by lakes and forests, Jensen took inspiration from the shapes he saw in nature – blossoms, leaves, flowing lines – which still echo through the brand's designs today. Georg Jensen's homeware collections range from sculptural pitchers to glassware and candle holders, perfect for creating a sense of *hygge* in the home. With a royal warrant from the Danish court and a reputation for understated elegance, the brand brings a quietly luxurious feel to everyday rituals. Over the years, Georg Jensen has collaborated with design icons including Arne Jacobsen, Patricia Urquiola and – more recently – the likes of Alfredo Häberli and Constantin Wortmann.

### H for HOUSE OF FINN JUHL

House of Finn Juhl is built around the legacy of one of Denmark's most influential mid-century designers. Originally trained as an architect, Finn Juhl started designing furniture in the 1940s with a totally fresh approach. At the vanguard of Scandinavian modernism, his pieces were organic, sculptural and full of character. With iconic designs including the famous Chieftain Chair and the colourful Glove Cabinet, he helped shape the Danish modern look we still love today. Finn Juhl died in 1989, but in 2001, Ivan Hansen and Hans Henrik Sørensen were entrusted with the rights to manufacture and relaunch his furniture. They co-founded House of Finn Juhl and have since worked tirelessly to relaunch over 50 of his masterpieces, including the Poet Sofa, Cocktail Table and Pelican Chair. Now, House of Finn Juhl continues to make his original designs using the same high level of craftsmanship. You'll find everything from his Egyptian and Reading Chairs to curvy sofas, elegant dining tables and beautifully made desks. Each piece has that signature mix of organic shape and thoughtful detail. UK retailers include Hyphen Design (hyphen-designagency.com).

▸ Amp up the chic in your home with these statement candle holders and vase, Georg Jensen. Available from black-by-design.co.uk

# The A–Z of Scandi brands

**IKEA is an affordable option for Scandi style, including this KLIPPAN sofa**

## I for IKEA

It's impossible to talk about Scandinavian design without mentioning IKEA. What started in the 1940s as a small mail-order business in the Swedish town of Älmhult is now one of the most recognisable home brands in the world. Founded by Ingvar Kamprad, IKEA's mission has always been simple: to make well-designed, functional furniture affordable for everyone. IKEA's influence on modern interiors is huge. It brought pared-back, functional design into the mainstream – think clean lines, pale woods, clever storage solutions – and made it possible to create a stylish home on a relative shoestring. Iconic pieces like the practical BILLY bookcase and the KLIPPAN sofa, with its modern, minimalist silhouette, have become staples around the globe. Remarkably, it's estimated that a BILLY bookcase is sold every five seconds. What sets IKEA apart is its commitment to 'democratic design': balancing form, function, quality, sustainability and price. It's thanks to this thoughtful yet accessible approach that the brand has maintained its global popularity.

## for JACOB JENSEN

Jacob Jensen Design is one of the quieter powerhouses of Danish design. Best known for its sleek, minimal aesthetic, the brand was founded by Jacob Jensen in the 1950s – a pioneering industrial designer who made his name creating iconic products in collaboration with Bang & Olufsen. His style was defined by clean lines, subtle contrasts, and a focus on function, setting the tone for a whole new wave of modernist design. Today, Jacob Jensen Design continues to produce everything from minimalist-style toasters and kettles to lighting and watches. The brand's design philosophy? To remove distractions and reveal the essential, turning ordinary interactions into extraordinary ones. Put simply, products are meticulously designed to make life easier and elevate the user experience, while embodying the principles of Nordic design: simplicity, functionality and timeless elegance. Everything feels carefully considered and beautifully restrained.

**Make breakfast in style with this modern kettle and toaster from Jacob Jensen**

**The Pelican Chair is a standout piece from House of Finn Juhl**

## K for KÄHLER

With a heritage stretching back to 1839, Kähler is one of Denmark's most enduring design names, built on decades of ceramic craftsmanship. What began as a small pottery workshop in the town of Næstved now creates dinnerware and vases loved across the world, thanks to its mix of tradition, artistry and Scandinavian style. Kähler is probably best known for its vases, especially the hand-painted Omaggio series, with its distinctive striped pattern, and the softly pleated Hammershøi collection, inspired by archive pieces. But the brand has evolved in recent years. For the kitchen, you'll find calm, functional tableware alongside elegant ceramic candle holders and sculptural serving pieces. The Urbania candle holders, shaped like tiny architectural buildings, add instant atmosphere, while collections like Nobili bring a quiet, Nordic take on seasonal Christmas decor.

## The A–Z of Scandi brands

### for LE KLINT

You can spot a Le Klint light a mile off – the delicate folds, soft glow and sculptural precision are part of what's made the Danish brand a design stalwart. Although officially founded in 1943, the brand's iconic pleated shade was created decades earlier for architect Peder Vilhelm Jensen-Klint's own home. What started as a family hobby evolved into a signature style, still hand-folded today in the brand's Odense studio. Le Klint's lamps are all about the craftsmanship: each shade is made by hand, using techniques passed down through generations. To become a pleating technician at Le Klint is no mean feat, for it takes around three years to fully master the skill. Collections like Swirl, with its flowing spiral form, and the Bouquet, a chandelier inspired by hanging flower buds, blend traditional folding with playful, sculptural shapes. More recent designs, like the minimal Caché or the soft, glowing Caleo, show how the brand continues to evolve while staying rooted in its history.

*Statement lighting from Le Klint can add focus to your home*

### for MØBEL COPENHAGEN

Møbel Copenhagen may be a relatively new name on the Danish design scene, but it is definitely one to watch. Founded in 2016 by Sara Agersborg, the studio blends classic design values like craftsmanship, functionality and honest materials, with a distinctly modern outlook. You'll find soft, sculptural seating, clever stacking stools and tables with beautifully considered details. Many designs are customisable too, with flexible finishes and materials that work across a range of spaces and styles. Each piece is made in close collaboration with skilled designers and makers, resulting in furniture that feels both thoughtful and bold. Current highlights include David Thulstrup's Taku chair, with its deeply curved back, Gry Holmskov's sculptural steel Angel stool, and the minimalist Lean sofa.

*This leather sofa from Møbel Copenhagen is available in a variety of colours*

### for NUURA

In Scandinavia, where winter days are short, lighting isn't just about visibility – it's also about comfort, atmosphere, and even mental wellbeing. Danish lighting studio Nuura, founded in 2017 by Sofie Refer, Nadia Lassen & Peter Østerberg, takes that seriously. The brand has rapidly built a name for itself thanks to its high-quality designs, often in finishes such as brass and ceramic. The name Nuura means 'light and honour', reflecting a quiet respect for the role light plays in everyday life, where it influences our circadian rhythm, energy, mood and health. From their base in Copenhagen, Nuura designs everything from hand-blown glass pendant lamps to chandeliers, table lamps and stylish cluster lamps. Their collections explore soft forms and subtle finishes, often drawing on organic shapes and Nordic natural beauty.

*Nuura's statement chandelier is simple but elegant*

Bring a pop of character to your home with OYOY's statement vase

## *for* **PAPPELINA**

In Scandinavia, the long-awaited arrival of summer brings with it a shift in lifestyle, as people embrace the changing weather. After cold, dark winters, there's a deep-rooted desire to be in nature, to feel the sun, and to make the most of the extended daylight. Pappelina's rugs fit naturally into this way of living. Made in Dalarna, Sweden, since 1999, the brand has become known for its low-maintenance, hardwearing rugs that work just as well in a hallway or kitchen as they do outside on a terrace, poolside, or even at the beach. Woven from phthalate-free and toxin-free PVC using traditional looms, they can be machine- and even pressure-washed. Many of the designs are inspired by nature, such as the URVI, which harks to the sea with its gentle wave patterns. Colour options in the Archipelago Collection nod to the breezy calm of the Swedish islands.

Pappelina's HILL rug in Brick is inspired by nature with its warm, earthy tones

## *for* **OYOY**

OYOY may be one of the newer names in Danish design, but since launching in 2012 it's quietly become a favourite for homes that value both style and warmth. Founded by designer Lotte Fynboe, the brand focuses on creating well-made, long-lasting homeware. Think everything from cushions and ceramics to woven rugs and wall hangings, with a profound emphasis on functionality and fun. There's plenty for children too, with a MINI range encompassing striped play mats, animal-shaped cushions and mobiles in muted tones. At the heart of OYOY's design ethos is a sense of play and an emphasis on comfort and aesthetics. The name OYOY itself is a nod to the brand's Danish heritage. The letters 'OY' have marked Danish aircraft since 1929, and here, it signals a connection to Denmark and a sense of belonging.

## *for* **ROYAL COPENHAGEN**

Royal Copenhagen celebrated its 250th anniversary in 2025, an impressive milestone indeed. Founded in 1775 and originally commissioned by the Danish royal family, this iconic porcelain brand has been part of the country's design language for centuries. Royal Copenhagen's pieces may be beautiful, but they are made to be used and appreciated, not just displayed. Its signature blue-and-white hand-painted patterns, often inspired by nature, grace tables across the world today. The Blue Fluted pattern, with its delicate florals and scrolling lines, is perhaps the most recognisable. But there are more contemporary designs too, like the wilder Blue Elements or Flora, which reinterpret the classic motifs with a more modern touch. Each piece is still hand-painted in Denmark and carries the brand's signature blue wave pattern on the back.

**Søstrene Grene's autumn range embraces warm natural tones and sculptural shapes**

### for SØSTRENE GRENE

One of our favourite places to snap up wallet-friendly Scandi homeware, Søstrene Grene has quietly built a loyal following – and not just for its alluring prices. Founded in Denmark in 1973, the family-owned brand blends function and charm, offering everything from brightly coloured mugs and candles to vases and salad servers, all with that Nordic balance of style and functionality. Their storage baskets, made from natural materials like bamboo, seagrass and willow, are perfect for calming clutter, while wooden pieces are crafted from FSC®-certified materials. With muted tones, simple shapes and that unmistakable Scandi knack for cosy minimalism, Søstrene Grene is ideal for creating *hygge* without overspending. Until recently, Søstrene Grene was a bit of a hidden gem, with only a handful of stores in the UK. But it unveiled its new flagship store off Oxford Street in 2025, and has ambitious plans to open 100 UK stores by 2027. The brand is also available to shop online.

## T *for* TORPLYKTAN

With roots in the forests of western Sweden, Torplyktan is a family-run brand with a deep connection to nature. Based in Västergötland, the company produces scented candles, diffusers and soaps that reflect the changing Nordic seasons. Scents pay homage to the natural world and are a reminder to slow down and savour the seasons, with collections inspired by everything from crisp Scandinavian pine woods to the Northern Lights and midnight sun. Ingredients are carefully sourced too, with clean-burning candles made from vegan, carbon-neutral soy wax from Sweden. Packaging also comes with a conscience – it's made from recycled materials and sourced from a local supplier.

**Umage offers both lighting and furniture in true Scandi style**

**Make your home smell like a pine forest**

## U *for* UMAGE

Scandinavian design often comes back to a few core ideas: simplicity, function, and a respect for nature. Danish brand Umage leans into all three, producing sculptural lampshades and thoughtfully designed furniture with a strong emphasis on style, sustainability and functionality. Best known for its feathered Eos lampshades and sculptural pendants like Clava Dine, Umage's lighting is designed to adapt, with the shades able to be used as pendants, table lamps or floor lights. That flexibility runs through their furniture too, where you'll find clever details – built-in charging ports, hidden storage – worked into minimalist forms. Umage means "to make an effort" in Danish, and that ethos manifests throughout the collection.

# V for VIPP

Vipp's story begins with a bin, but not just any bin. Created in 1939 by Holger Nielsen for his wife's hair salon, the original Vipp pedal bin was built to last, with a simplicity and sturdiness that still defines the brand today. It's earned a spot in the Museum of Modern Art's permanent design collection, but Vipp has long since moved beyond its utilitarian origins. Still family-owned and run from Copenhagen, Vipp now produces a full range of furniture, kitchens, lighting and bathroom pieces. Much of it follows the same logic as the original bin: solid materials, minimal fuss and a sense that function doesn't have to compromise form. You'll find stainless steel, powder-coated metal and matte finishes throughout – an industrial edge, softened by careful detailing. It's a brand that has stayed close to its roots, even as its collection has grown to include everything from modular kitchens to soft lighting and sleek, understated seating. For an immersive experience, you can even stay at one of the brand's guesthouses, such as the Vipp Shelter at Lake Immeln in Sweden.

*Vipp has remained true to its roots, proving function doesn't have to compromise form*

# for WARM NORDIC

Founded by Frantz Longhi, Danish brand Warm Nordic looks after the design heritage of world-renowned icons such as Hans Olsen, Knud Færch and Arne Hovmand-Olsen. Collections are split between old and new: the Classic line and the Contemporary collection. While the Contemporary line works with designers to create new pieces, the Classic collection focuses on relaunching designs from the 1950s and 60s that deserve icon status. Working in close collaboration with the designers' families, the brand recreates classic furniture and lamps, such as the Fried Egg Chair, in modern colours and materials. Among the most recognisable pieces is the Beak Bird, a series of wooden bird sculptures first designed in 1961 by Svend Aage Holm-Sørensen.

*Warm Nordic embraces both old and new designs in their product lines*

# Z for ZONE DENMARK

Zone Denmark is one of those businesses that quietly improves everyday life with its elegant yet functional pieces, produced in collaboration with a hand-picked team of Danish designers. The products – which cover everything from soap dispensers and pedal bins to kitchen tools, mirrors and lighting – are super stylish, but always with a thoughtful edge. Zone Denmark has multiple international design awards under its belt, thanks to its innovative approach. Each piece is designed to challenge convention in subtle ways – whether it's a folding stool, a cordless lamp or a stackable dish – while still fitting seamlessly into everyday routines.

# Scandi Christmas

**Future PLC** Quay House, The Ambury, Bath, BA1 1UA

### Editorial
Group Editor **Philippa Grafton**
Art Editor **Katy Stokes**
Head of Art & Design **Greg Whitaker**
Editorial Director **Jon White**
Managing Director **Grainne McKenna**

### Ideal Home Editorial
Editor-in-Chief **Heather Young**
Creative Director **Emma Williams**

### Cover image
Mary Wadsworth

### Photography
All copyrights and trademarks are recognised and respected

### Advertising
Media packs are available on request
Commercial Director **Clare Dove**

### International
Head of Print Licensing **Rachel Shaw**
licensing@futurenet.com
www.futurecontenthub.com

### Circulation
Head of Newstrade **Tim Mathers**

### Production
Head of Production **Mark Constance**
Production Project Manager **Matthew Eglinton**
Advertising Production Manager **Joanne Crosby**
Digital Editions Controller **Jason Hudson**
Production Managers **Keely Miller, Nola Cokely, Vivienne Calvert, Fran Twentyman**

Printed in the UK

**Distributed by** Marketforce – www.marketforce.co.uk
For enquiries, please email: mfcommunications@futurenet.com

**GPSR EU RP (for authorities only)**
eucomply OÜ Pärnu mnt 139b-14 11317, Tallinn, Estonia
hello@eucompliancepartner.com, +3375690241

**Scandi Christmas First Edition (HOB7612)**
© 2025 Future Publishing Limited

We are committed to only using magazine paper which is derived from responsibly managed, certified forestry and chlorine-free manufacture. The paper in this bookazine was sourced and produced from sustainable managed forests, conforming to strict environmental and socioeconomic standards.

All contents © 2025 Future Publishing Limited or published under licence. All rights reserved. No part of this magazine may be used, stored, transmitted or reproduced in any way without the prior written permission of the publisher. Future Publishing Limited (company number 2008885) is registered in England and Wales. Registered office: Quay House, The Ambury, Bath BA1 1UA. All information contained in this publication is for information only and is, as far as we are aware, correct at the time of going to press. Future cannot accept any responsibility for errors or inaccuracies in such information. You are advised to contact manufacturers and retailers directly with regard to the price of products/services referred to in this publication. Apps and websites mentioned in this publication are not under our control. We are not responsible for their contents or any other changes or updates to them. This magazine is fully independent and not affiliated in any way with the companies mentioned herein.

Future plc is a public company quoted on the London Stock Exchange (symbol: FUTR)
www.futureplc.com

Chief Executive Officer **Kevin Li Ying**
Non-Executive Chairman **Richard Huntingford**
Chief Financial Officer **Sharjeel Suleman**

Tel +44 (0)1225 442 244

Part of the

bookazine series